ty TEACH YOURSELF

WINNING AT
JOB INTERVIEWS

TEACH YOURSELF

WINNING AT
JOB INTERVIEWS

Igor S. Popovich

Hodder & Stoughton

A MEMBER OF THE HODDER HEADLINE GROUP

British Library Cataloguing in Publication Data

Popovich, Igor S.
  Winning at Job Interviews
  I. Title
  650.14
  ISBN 0-340-61858-2

First published in 1994·
Impression number   10 9 8 7 6 5
Year   1999 1998 1997

The 'Teach Yourself' name and logo are registered trade marks of
Hodder & Stoughton Ltd in the UK.

Typeset by Rowland Phototypesetting Limited,
Bury St Edmunds, Suffolk.
Printed in Great Britain for Hodder and Stoughton Educational,
a division of Hodder Headline Plc, 338 Euston Road, London NW13BH
by Cox & Wyman Limted, Cardiff Rd, Reading, Berks.

———— CONTENTS ————

– ABOUT THE AUTHOR –

Igor S. Popovich was born in 1962 in Yugoslavia. He finished high school in 1981 and after the compulsory one-year National Service in Marine Troops he enrolled at The University of Zagreb. In 1986 he graduated with honours at The Faculty of Engineering, majoring in Industrial Electronics.

He started his professional career as a research engineer and lecturer at The University of Osijek, in his home town of Osijek. Due to the difficult economic and unstable political situation in the country at the time, in April 1988 he migrated to Perth, Australia.

As an Instrumentation Engineer in the oil and gas industry, working for Exploration Logging of Australia, he travelled across Australia, Singapore and New Zealand. In 1990 he joined one of Australia's biggest companies, Western Mining Corporation, at their nickel and gold operations in Leinster, WA, with intentions of gaining experience in mining and mineral processing industry. In late 1991 he accepted a more senior position with BHP, the biggest Australian company.

His interests are broad. Interior design, travel, music, literature, and, above all, human nature and interactions between people.

As a director of a career-help consultancy, he organises and runs training courses on employment interviewing, job hunting and career management.

Also by the author: *Your Job – How To Get It, How To Keep It*, Simon & Schuster.

— DEDICATION —

To my parents,
Slobodan and Ela,
for their love and support
through all those years of sacrifice.

— INTRODUCTION —

The future never just happened. It was created.

Will and Ariel Durant, *The Lessons of History*

_____ What they do teach you _____
at university

I started my university studies in the early eighties. I was keen, I studied hard and my grades were excellent. Sometimes it was fun, but it was never easy. Some people found it too difficult, but I was prepared for the five years of hard work.

In the introductory lecture, one of the professors said to more than 450 freshmen: 'Today you are entering the Faculty of Electrical Engineering. It is one of the most reputable Schools in the country. The degrees obtained here are recognised in most western countries and are highly regarded by employers.

'You will have to master a range of different subjects, you'll have to pass calculus, differential equations, statistics, solid state physics, and other difficult courses. Take my word for it, you'll learn engineering and you'll enjoy it. But don't fool yourselves: it won't be easy to get there. I'll give you an idea of how difficult it is going to be. I want you to take a good look at the person on your left and at the person on your right. Only one of you will become a graduate engineer.'

All of his predictions came true, except one – the electrical engineering program was dull and hostile to our young minds and I didn't enjoy it. All I enjoyed was the relief after passing the exams. Every time I passed one, I would feel closer to my ultimate goal. It was almost like our lecturers had a boot camp mentality: 'I went through it, now you've got to go through it.'

I will never forget the day I did the presentation of my thesis and received the official certificate (the graduation ceremony took place two months later). I felt like I was on the top of the world. All my dreams came true and all that hard work came into fruition: I became **somebody**! The world was my oyster. I managed to get a job as a research and development engineer and part-time lecturer at the local university in my home town. I had plenty of free time to pursue my interests. English was one of them. That's when the idea to move to Australia was born. When I arrived in 1988, a whole range of new opportunities opened in front of me. But things were not that easy in the beginning. All that glittered wasn't gold!

____ What they don't teach you at ____ university

It took me about two years to realise how little I knew. Not about electrical engineering, but about the real world. Hundreds of vacant jobs in the local paper every Saturday lured me into thinking that getting the right one would be a piece of cake. The only problem was that I didn't know how to go about it, or where to start. The whole system was new to me: jobs, résumés, interviews, employment agencies, application letters, competition . . .

With a little help from my friends, I soon mastered the skill for what proved to be the second biggest challenge in my life: the art of getting a job and keeping it. Keeping it was relatively easy, the first part was the tricky one. After more than two hundred applications and about twenty interviews, I finally landed my first professional job. Since I'm one of those people who constantly seeks something better, more challenging and more rewarding, in the following four years I changed jobs four times and moved three times.

Each subsequent job was easier to get than the previous ones. I had a good command of the English language, relevant local experience, relatively good references, and, above all, I knew how to sell myself and how to be 'The One' among forty or more engineers who applied for the same jobs.

Nobody taught me how to do it, I had to learn the hard way – through my own experience. Much later I discovered self-improvement books. They became my best allies and helped me reinforce my knowledge of the job-finding process and various related areas: communicating with people, negotiating, public speaking, selling techniques, technical and business writing, management methods, leadership and many others.

— The importance of neglected skills —

It took me more than twenty-five years to realise the simple truth about the most valuable skills in life. Those are the so-called 'broad' or 'generalist' skills. The most important among them is definitely the ability to relate to people and to communicate with them through speech, manners, body language and writing.

They are the skills that can and, if you possess them, will get you employed and keep you there. The sad truth is that you won't learn how to acquire or improve them in school. The only way to do that is through your own efforts. This book should help you to bridge that gap in your education.

Very early in the job-hunting process I developed a habit: after each unsuccessful interview I would write down everything I could remember about it: the questions, the interviewer's style, behaviour and comments, names and facts, figures and impressions.

Very slowly, a pattern started to emerge. Some questions were repeated more often than others and I began to recognise the mistakes I made in each particular case: wrong answers, wrong gestures, inappropriate questions, poor posture.

As I was improving my résumé and my performance at the interviews, the recession was spreading at an unprecedented pace and getting the right job was becoming more and more difficult. My newly acquired skills were put to harder and harder tests each time I applied for a job. That was when the idea of writing this book was born. Unemployment broke the 10 per cent barrier, and I felt that was the time to share my experiences with other job hunters, who, like myself, were constantly searching for the 'magic' wand that will get them the elusive job of their dreams.

My book is now in your hands. For the next few hundred pages I'll lead you through the strange world of employment interviewing. As happens in life, you may not agree with everything I say. That's perfectly normal, I don't expect you to. The main purpose of the book is to start you thinking about employment interviews and to give you a foundation for using your own ideas, methods and tactics in interviewing.

— My reasons for writing this book —

Being a Libran, I have always highly valued justice, fairness and individual achievements. My engineering degree reinforced my belief in logic and reason. Later I realised that the real world is hardly based on logic. It is based on feelings.

Furthermore, I have always had sympathy for the individuals who never surrender, for the fighters who constantly try to change things for the better and challenge the system, particularly if it's wrong.

Combining all those traits, one can hardly be surprised by my desire to help the amateur job seekers who are severely disadvantaged in their dealings with professional players in the job game: recruiters, personnel officers and employment consultants.

On a more general scale, most problems stem from the fact that people deal with 'professionals' in every sphere of their lives. Recruiters, doctors, real-estate agents, lawyers, used car salesmen, bank managers, government clerks, accountants and other professional 'users and abusers' have a distinct advantage over most people, so they can (and do) manipulate us (the unwary amateurs) in the process. The onus is on the users of those services (in this case, the job hunters) to educate themselves in various areas and protect their interests.

You had better learn how to swim with the sharks, or risk being eaten alive!

The purpose of this book

After studying this book and applying the acquired knowledge at interviews, you will not automatically become an expert in interviewing, but your chances for success in dealing with employers will skyrocket and give you a distinct advantage over your competitors.

Teach Yourself Winning at Job Interviews is my contribution to your education. By reading it, you are taking a giant step towards success in job hunting. You may agree or disagree with some of my views and recommendations. Some tactics may work for you, others may not. The final judgement will be yours.

Should you find this book useful in your interviewing, recommend it to your friends who are looking for a job. They will probably be grateful to you for sharing your 'secrets' with them.

Your success will be easy to measure: you will either get a job or you won't. The measure of my success will be the fact that this book has found its way to people who need advice, and has helped them to get the desired job. In that case, I would consider my mission accomplished.

It is much more difficult to get a job than to keep it.

—— The people who get ahead ——

The world we live in is not based on logic, justice or equality. These are just the ideals we humans have been trying to achieve for ages. Apart from our efforts, knowledge and hard work, our success also depends on emotions, luck, and interaction between people. That's probably one of the reasons why the best, the smartest and the most capable people are not always at the top. (There are some exceptions to this rule, fortunately.)

> *The people who get ahead are not necessarily smarter.*
> *They simply have a better understanding of their influence*
> *and are not afraid to exercise it. While their rivals are*
> *making a recommendation, the winners are already in*
> *action.*
>
> M. H. McCormack, *The 110% Solution*

As a direct consequence, the world is not as good as it could be. Middle class is rapidly disappearing in today's society. In other words: the rich are getting richer and the poor are becoming even poorer.

Let's start by asking a simple question: What could an ordinary person, like you or me, do to stay on the brighter side of the street?

Unfortunately, the answer to that question is not so simple. Hundreds of books have been written in the effort to solve one or more pieces of this puzzle. There are literally thousands of self-improvement books at your disposal, dealing with a great variety of subjects, all trying to help you achieve your goals, no matter what they are.

> *There is only one success in life: to be able to live your life*
> *the way you want.*
>
> Christopher Morley

Strategies for success

I believe that all available facts, tactics and strategies for success could be summarised in the following five point advice on how to get ahead in life:

- Get as much education and acquire as much knowledge and know-how as possible.
- Find an interesting, well-paying job with good career prospects.
- Mix with successful people and use them to climb the corporate and social ladder.
- Invest your hard earned money wisely and create a 'nest egg' for retirement.
- Retire after accumulating an amount of money that will enable you to 'live comfortably ever after'.

This may sound simple or trivial, but you would be surprised by how many people fail to achieve even one of those five goals. The tricky thing is that the achievement of each step is usually a prerequisite for the next one. It's like climbing a ladder. The safest and easiest way is not to jump steps, otherwise you may end up like numerous fallen entrepreneurial stars: in court, bankrupt, in jail, or all three.

Getting professional help

On the road to success you'll meet various people who may help you achieve your goals, such as accountants, financial advisers, bank managers, lawyers and the like. Some of them are honest, hard-working people who can give you the right advice and help you immensely.

But, beware, like in any trade, there are some con artists around. They can hardly wait to rip you off and use your fees to buy a new set of sheepskin seat covers for their Volvos and BMWs.

All professions are conspiracies against the laity.

George Bernard Shaw

—— Finding a job ——

Now we tackle the second step on the road to success! You have probably asked yourself what is so difficult about getting the right job? It is that most of the time, no one else can help you to get the job of your dreams. You will have to do it on your own. (As for any rule, there are some exceptions here – if your father is the General Manager or Chief Executive Officer, this may not apply to you!)

But, you'll say, I can get some help from employment agencies, résumé preparation services, friends who can recommend me to their employers, and so on. That's true, but keep in mind that **you** will have to do most of the work to get a good job. Nobody will bring it to you on a silver plate.

—— Doing it yourself ——

Nobody can make a good career plan for you, nor can anyone else attend a job interview in your place. You will be there on your own, so, with the help of *Teach Yourself Winning at Job Interviews*, you had better prepare yourself for the challenge.

> ***There are two times in life when you are totally alone: just before you die and just before you go in for a job interview.***

In this book we will talk about career management. However, due to the complexity of the subject and the fact that all aspects can not be covered in a single book (if the job is done properly), we will focus our attention on one of the most important steps (if not **the** most important one) in the job-hunting process – the job interview!

I bet the mere thought of a job interview makes your palms sweat and your pulse race. I believe the reason for such a reaction is because subconsciously you recognise the importance of the event. Your whole career and future life may depend upon the outcome of a single job interview, on whether or not you will get that particular job, the one that can enhance your chances of achieving success!

Job interviews

You obviously recognise the importance of a job interview, otherwise you would not be reading this book right now. The rules, principles and examples outlined are based on real life situations, common sense and a lot of research by experts. The text is easy to follow and you do not need the knowledge of calculus, cash flow analysis, or a PhD in psychology. All you need is honesty with yourself, an honest desire to improve, keen determination and, as is usual in life, some luck.

You will probably want to ask if the tactics and strategies outlined in this book always work. They don't. Nothing does. But they will be the closest you can get to the 'magic wand'.

There is no panacea, or universal recipe, that works every time. Every job interview is different and the whole process is influenced by many factors that can make an impact on the final outcome. But, by following certain rules and doing your preparations properly, you can gain control over most of these obstacles and traps for the unwary.

Because interviews are so predictable, they are controllable!

If you prepare yourself for the questions you'll be asked, if you deliver the right answers in the right manner and if you project a positive image of yourself, your chances of getting the job you want will improve dramatically!

There is only a limited number of questions that you can be asked to answer during a job interview. Most interviewers will ask you the same questions because what they want to hear are the same right answers. It is your job to provide the right answers. That is why the skeleton of your answers should remain unchanged. I have produced those skeletons for you. Don't change them radically. Adjust them to suit your situation and, if needed, add the necessary information to complement them.

Of course, the words, accent and tone of voice interviewers will use to ask those questions will vary with each case. These are the minor variations and they make the job of answering those cliché questions more interesting.

_____ How to get the most out of _____ this book

You have already made the first and most difficult step towards successful interviewing – you have recognised the need to improve your interviewing skills. Every step that follows will be easier to master if you follow some basic rules. The main point you have to remember is that it is impossible to master any skill by merely reading how to do it. You have to practise – by yourself first, then with a friend or a relative, and finally at real interviews. Each unsuccessful interview will be a lesson to remember. Don't consider it a failure. If you learn just one simple truth per interview, you'll be one step closer to your goal.

These are my suggestions on how to use this book:

- Read the whole book once or twice, marking those questions in Chapter 6 that could possibly apply to your situation and are relevant to you.
- Do a complete and honest evaluation of yourself, your strengths and weaknesses. If you haven't done this already, before writing your résumé, this is the last chance to do it. Identify the critical points and make a plan of action for rectifying or neutralising the bad ones and emphasising and reinforcing the good ones.
- Do a thorough search on the particular employer. Use all known facts in the preparation of your answers. This will enable you to show your knowledge of the company and create a positive impression.
- Customise the answers to suit your particular case and the job you will be interviewed for.

- Practise answering the questions. The more time you devote to practise, the more successful you'll be. You can even record the questions and answers on cassette and play it over and over until it 'sits' in your mind, or get a friend or relative to videotape you while you answer the questions, or to play the role of the interviewer. That would help you evaluate and correct not only your answers and tone of voice, but also your posture, gestures and body language! Don't worry about over-rehearsing. Even if you know the answers 'by heart', there is no danger that you will sound superficial. You will keep changing your tone and pitch of voice naturally, because your sub-conscious mind will be telling you to do so.

The question of ethics

If you feel that preparing yourself for the interview, customising your answers to suit the occasion (which is different from lying), and using appropriate tactics to counteract the ones interviewers use may not be ethical or fair, think again. If you want to stay poor or unemployed, fine. If not, you had better adopt some guerilla tactics.

The end justifies the means.

Niccolo Machiavelli

This book will not teach you how to cheat, lie and blatantly falsify your answers. I strongly disagree with those methods and advise you not to use them as your modus operandi. Despite Machiavelli's quotation, there is no end that can justify all the means.

There is a difference between lying and telling the interviewers what they want to hear. In the latter case you just disclose the information that will improve your chances and avoid unveiling anything that can have a negative impact on the interviewers.

Despite the fact that glibness and prevarication shouldn't be used at a job interview, as many as one quarter of all applicants can be expected to cheat. According to J P McAward, president of a New York investigating agency, McAward Associates, 'about 25 per cent of job candidates can be expected to falsify their answers to some application questions. The most misrepresented is the individual's employment record. Typical falsifications: The individuals don't hold the jobs described; their salaries were not as high as claimed; major difficulties with superiors are completely covered up.'

There is a big difference between falsifying your answers and using the tactics outlined in this book. I will summarise them for you. Remember them well and apply them in your interviews. The results will surprise you.

- Never disclose any negative information about yourself voluntarily.
- When asked about your weaknesses, mistakes and other negative information, use the least detrimental case as an example and quickly switch to the corrective action you've taken, improvements and strong points in that area.
- Always listen for the clues that will tell what interviewers want to hear, then tell them exactly that. If that calls for 'modifying' the truth, try to look at it from a different perspective. If you haven't actually done something, but know how to do it, transform your theoretical answers into actual experience. Employers are seldom interested in 'would do' or 'could do' answers. They want details about your specific experience. Don't let them down. If they are happy with your answer, what difference does the fact that you haven't actually done it make? None for them, because you know how to do it and could do it if needed, and bully for you, because it could get you a job you want!

1

WHAT ARE ——— EMPLOYERS ——— LOOKING FOR?

——— Recessionary times ———

Employers

We are living in recessionary times. Energetic companies these days make it hard to get hired. They deliberately understaff their operations and use contractors and part-time employees to cater for peak periods in the business cycle. Recruitment professionals develop detailed selection criteria for each and every position and pay special attention to employing the right people.

The balance of power has shifted completely in favour of employers. With an average of forty to sixty applicants for most professional positions and more than a hundred for other jobs, guess who is dictating the terms?

The global lack of vision and strategic planning on the part of employers is obvious. They take on new people during upsurges in business, then lay them off when business starts to decline. This is augmented by the common 'last in, first out' practice, which can leave job seekers with erratic looking résumés and can seriously damage their prospects of gaining employment.

The buyer's market is enabling employers to dictate terms and freeze (or even reduce) salaries and available benefits. To save money, more and more companies are hiring from the 'bottom of the stack', instead of from the top. By doing that, they are not getting top value for their money. Ten per cent higher salary could mean one hundred per cent better performance.

The current trends among employers are emphasising more flexible hiring methods, in order to find multi-skilled, adaptable employees who will assume responsibility and accept rapid changes in the work force.

Employees

High unemployment has an impact on the way employees behave. It creates a timid and compliant work force. Workers fear their employers and the possibility of losing their jobs. This phenomenon is primarily noticeable in less-unionised professions.

To keep our jobs, we'll have to work harder, longer hours (as long as necessary to accomplish the tasks) and perform virtually any task, whether or not we were trained for it, all for the same or less money than people earn in non-recessionary times. Jobs are scarce and many careers have been stalled or disrupted by retrenchments, redundancies, lay-offs and restructuring.

Restructuring

Restructuring efforts are viewed by employers as the first step towards building a productive and reliable work force and abandoning restricted work practices. Such practices and inefficiencies have been eroding economies for decades.

Restructuring of the work force results in greater emphasis on multi-skilled workers and less on specific credentials and narrowly defined jobs. Transferable skills, such as oral and written communication skills and inter-personal and people management skills, are gaining importance in the eyes of employers. Because of the difficulty in predicting future trends in the economy and labour market, flexibility and willingness to change are viewed by employers as highly desirable qualities.

Most employers will never employ staff at the levels experienced before the last recession. Some jobs have disappeared for good. Voluntary redundancy schemes are gaining popularity among employers who are trying to change the structure of jobs and decrease the number of employees.

Voluntary or forced redundancy payments are perceived as highly attractive by some employees. The number of people wanting to take advantage of the packages usually exceeds by far the number of packages available. The possible explanation is that most people believe that it's better to be retrenched now, with a nice payment in the pocket, than to be sacked without any severance pay in a few months' time, when the crisis deepens even further. I couldn't agree more, but the important issue here is the employers' point of view. Their strategies, policies and philosophies, reflected in the hiring process, will directly or indirectly affect you and your future prospects in the job market.

Times are tough and will get even tougher. This calls for immediate and drastic action on everybody's part. Employers are getting lean and mean. You had better follow that path, too.

———— Career and job security ————

In the Western world, which generally operates according to the principle of supply and demand, the following factors determine how much we get paid:

- the demand for the type of job we do;
- how well we do our jobs;
- how difficult it would be to replace us.

As one of the results of the rapid changes in the way modern companies operate in a harsh economic climate, long-term employment is rapidly disappearing, leaving those unprepared for such a change in total confusion. We simply cannot rely on our employers to take care of us until we retire.

Therefore, the only security you can count on has to come from within yourself. It is based on your knowledge, skills and know-how. In order to succeed in life you have to take time and make an effort to improve your education and acquire skills that are in demand by employers. In today's business climate, one point has to be emphasised.

There is no such thing as a secure job!

Some naïve players in the job game think that their jobs are 'for life'. This sense of security comes from the perceived balance of power that existed in the past. They falsely presume that:

- their jobs won't change;
- their jobs will always exist;
- the employers will feel grateful for their (the employee's) achievements in the past;
- the employers will take care of their careers, promote them and reward them for a job well done;
- if they lose their job, the employer will re-employ them as soon as the hard times are over.

The reality is very different. In today's world employers are interested only in their profits and in returns to shareholders and investors. Whole lines of management are disappearing, professionals (engineers, lawyers, accountants) are being retrenched, as well as blue collar workers; the axe is falling on all layers of the corporate structure.

So, like it or not, you had better start to like living dangerously. If you don't already enjoy it, force yourself to accept challenge and uncertainty. Try to conquer the symptoms of an 'ostrich syndrome'. Don't bury your head in the sand! You can use it for better purposes – to observe the job market around you, note the trends, make conclusions and plan your actions.

Testing the job market

Instead of spending hours at the weekend reading the sports pages in the newspapers, devote an hour or two to scanning employment advertisements, even if you are employed. This will give you an idea about what's happening in the job market. You may be pleasantly surprised if you discover that there is a healthy demand for people with qualifications and experience similar to yours.

You can even go a step further. If you are not sure about your value or your career prospects, apply for a few jobs just to probe the market! Some less reputable employers do it, too. Although they are not allowed (by law) to use this method of 'market research', employers sometimes advertise for non-existent positions to get a better idea about the job market for certain groups of employees. That helps them in salary reviews, in dealings with unions and in other strategies used to keep the balance of power in their favour.

You have an advantage over employers in this area, because it is perfectly legal to apply for a job without any intention of eventually accepting the offer. Even if you are not thinking about changing jobs, this exercise can give you a sense of reality and assist you in putting a price tag on yourself. You could be worth more than you think!

Managing your career

Fortune magazine columnist Walter Kiechel advises job hunters to jump at jobs with other companies whenever the opportunity arises, because when they are forced to leave their present employers, those jobs may not be vacant any more. For him, the 'New Employment Contract' holds that: *Hereinafter, the employee will assume full responsibility for his own career – for keeping his qualifications up to date, for getting himself moved to the next position at the right time, for salting away funds for retirement, and, most daunting of all, for achieving job satisfaction. The company, while making no promises, will endeavour to provide a conducive environment, economic exigencies permitting.*

So, if security no longer comes from being employed, where does it come from? From being **employable**! Employability security is the new watchword. It means that you should:

- accumulate knowledge, skills and a reputation that can easily be transferred to other companies and invested in new opportunities;

- try to master 'portable skills', those that will be demanded by other employers because they could easily be applied in various corporate environments;
- ask yourself about every assignment, every project – 'How will this experience benefit my career prospects?' and 'How is it going to look on my résumé?';
- stay in touch with influential people outside your present employer, people who can help you in finding a job should the need arise. Cultivate your relationships with recruiters and employment agencies. You'll need them to help you in your job-hunting efforts;
- remain visible, mobile and credible. Do not overspecialise. Keep all your options open.

The ideal employee

> *As a personnel management trainee, I was told the perfect advertisement was the one which drew one reply and that was from the ideal candidate.*

Len Peach, *The Times*, 29 August 1985

Skills in demand

If you ask ten employers to define an ideal employee, it is very likely that you will get ten different answers. Each interviewer has his/her own ideas about the people they would like to employ. The traits that are extremely important in some positions may not be very relevant for other jobs. To illustrate these differences we'll use three common jobs – computer programmer, secretary and design engineer – as examples. For each of these positions the critical success factors differ:

Criteria for choosing a Computer Programmer

- knowledge of particular computing environments (OS/2, DOS, UNIX, CPM, Windows . . .);
- working knowledge of operating systems, knowledge of programming languages and software packages;

- attention to detail;
- mathematical/analytical skills;
- appropriate work standards;
- good communication skills;
- appropriate keyboard skills.

Criteria for choosing a Secretary

- typing speed (words per minute);
- shorthand skills;
- ability to use word processing packages and personal computers;
- strong interpersonal and communication skills;
- good grammar, editing and proof-reading skills;
- sensitivity;
- initiative, ability to learn;
- cooperation and teamwork.

Criteria for choosing a Design Engineer

- knowledge of relevant standards, regulations and work practices;
- ability to work alone and in a team environment;
- good technical knowledge of the required discipline;
- drafting skills;
- estimating and budgeting skills;
- attention to detail;
- high work standards;
- effective oral and written communication skills.

Despite the differences in these criteria, there are some qualities that are highly regarded by employers and therefore well sought after. With those qualities in mind, the ideal employee should be:

- mature and responsible;
- competent;
- trained and experienced;
- a good communicator;
- a good motivator;
- a self-starter;
- able to work alone and in a team;
- loyal;
- mentally and physically healthy;

- easy to work with;
- highly ethical and of high integrity;
- self-motivated.

Interviewers' fears

To be successful in the interview, you have to realise that interviewers are almost as nervous, anxious and confused as the applicants themselves. By asking each question, they try to find an answer to one of their fears and concerns. You, the candidate, have to frame your answers accordingly, address those aspects and convince employers that their fears are without foundation; in other words, that you are a good investment of their time and money.

What are the employers' major fears?

1   Employee won't be able to do the job, owing to lack of necessary skills or experience.

2   Employee won't be self-motivated.

3   Employee will frequently be on sick leave.

4   Employee will only stay around for a short time and then resign as soon as a better opportunity arises.

5   Employee will take too long to learn the job and to become a profitable investment.

6   Employee won't get along well with his co-workers and the management.

7   Employee will only do the absolute minimum he can get away with, rather than the maximum he is capable of.

8   Employee will bring discredit upon his boss and the whole department.

There are three basic groups of people. Some people make things happen, some watch things happen and some wonder what happened. Employers want to employ people who make things happen, not passive bystanders.

In your answers, project the 'I'm a person of action' attitude.

Job descriptions and selection criteria

When preparing for a job interview, the first prerequisite is to identify the most sought after qualities by the particular employer in your field of work. You should base your performance on those factors in order to impress the head-hunters.

Sometimes it may be possible to get hold of job descriptions or selection criteria from your prospective employer. Some big companies use them, but public companies and Government departments are particularly inclined towards them. In most cases the applicants have to address the selection criteria in their applications. The same applies for the interview.

By making selection criteria available to applicants, employers try to scare off the less qualified or less experienced candidates. But they also help some shrewd professional interviewees to frame their interview presentations accordingly.

_____ Doing your homework _____ on employers

The two most important things in any business do not appear on its balance sheet – they are its People and its Reputation.

Henry Ford

Ideally, you should start doing your research on the potential employers even before you send your résumé to them. That way you can frame your application to suit each particular employer's circumstances, their way of thinking and operating and, most importantly, their selection criteria. If you are invited for an interview, the importance of getting to know the employer skyrockets.

As you expand your knowledge of the employer, the balance of power shifts in your favour.

If you are able to show the interviewers that you have done some research on them and that you know a lot about their operations, they are very likely to think: 'If he went to all that trouble to find out details about us before the interview, can you imagine what he could do for us if we employ him? This is the person we want on our team!'.

You can show your knowledge through pertinent statements, smart and appropriate questions and properly framed answers to their questions. Don't try to 'look smart' or convince the interviewers that you have done research on their companies. Let them realise that themselves.

The question in front of us now is how to approach the whole investigation process? The answer is: by following the basic steps outlined below.

1   Information gathering. This is the most tedious and time-consuming task, but it pays high interest!

2   Screening the facts and selecting the relevant information. Easier than the previous step and much more interesting.

3   Using the relevant facts to frame your answers. The best answers, given in Chapter 6, should be expanded and slightly modified to suit your particular case, and each employer. Always keep in mind one rule: tell them what they want to hear!

There are various methods and tactics that could help you to do your homework on the potential employers. Some of them will prove invaluable, for the information you gather may make the difference between success and failure at the interview. Let's take a quick look at the sources of information and methods of using it.

Scanning the available literature

The time spent in a library could prove your best investment in the employment-searching procedure. Trade and financial magazines and publications are an excellent source of information. Annual reports, brochures, pamphlets and newsletters published by the companies could be even more valuable to a job seeker.

As a general suggestion, I would advise you to establish your own databank on major employers in your field. Collect all articles from newspapers and magazines and other printed materials, job advertisements, etc. Establish a filing system for easy reference and updating.

Using your friends and acquaintances as sources of information

Friends and relatives can provide you with specific, inside information about companies they work for, or through them you can meet people who work for the companies you are interviewing with. Inside information is valuable and would certainly give you an edge over other candidates, if used in the right way.

However, once at the interview, do not mention your friends or acquaintances. You don't know how good (or bad) the personal relationship between the interviewer and your friend is, so you could do your prospects some serious damage.

Using your business contacts

If you plan to stay within the industry you are already in, your business contacts could provide even more detailed inside information. They will know most corporate games, plans and developments, so, depending on the nature of your relationship with them, they could dispense some information to you. Always foster a good relationship with your former employers, customers, suppliers, etc. You never know when you are going to need them.

Contact the prospective employers

Before the interview, contact the receptionist or the interviewer's secretary by phone, or go to see them personally. The best time for this is when arranging the interview. Use the opportunity to ask questions about the interviewer(s), their names, titles, positions, backgrounds, etc. Formulate your questions carefully, so you don't sound too pushy or nosey.

Try to establish friendly contact with the secretaries and receptionists. Quite often interviewers ask them for an opinion on the candidates, or about their impression of applicants when they approach the desk.

When you talk to people on the phone, they are not usually the ones who will interview you. If they ask why you want to know details, you can say that you don't want to appear unprepared at the interview and that you don't want to waste anybody's time if you're not qualified. Of course, you don't want to waste your precious time if you're over-qualified, either.

The best tactic would be to go to see the receptionist or secretary in person. They usually appreciate a little chat if you show genuine interest in them and their company. It is very easy to dismiss a faceless voice over the phone. In a face-to-face meeting, they are more likely to help you.

The worst possible feeling at the interview is the one when you don't know who your interviewers are, what roles they play in the company, or what they expect from the candidates. In most cases the first and last time most job applicants hear their interviewers' names and titles is at the beginning of the interview, when they introduce themselves. Most candidates are either very nervous at that stage or they try to make a good impression on the interviewers, so they concentrate on how to introduce themselves and don't even get the names right. Never, ever start an interview without knowing who your interviewers are and where they fit in the company's structure.

Classifying information

The information you obtain from the sources listed above will cover all aspects of the prospective employer. Your next task will be to classify the available data into categories. This will enable you to systematise your knowledge of the employer and help you to use the facts to your advantage. So what are the areas you would be looking at? What questions do you have to find answers for? Here are some of the most important:

Services and products produced by the company

Does the company provide services, products or both?
What type of products or services?
How many different products or services are produced?
Which products or services are the most profitable or have the greatest potential?
How are the products produced or services provided? What manufacturing methods are used?
What quality control techniques are used?

Company's customers and markets

Who are the company's main customers?
How good is the relationship between the company and its customers?
What is the history of that relationship? What are the present and future trends?
What are the firm's plans in the areas of marketing, gaining new markets or expanding the existing ones?

Organisational aspects of the company

How is the company organised? What is the function of each department?
How many layers of management does the company have? What are they?
What are the main areas of responsibility for each level?
Which departments generate profit? Which departments are not so successful?
What are the opportunities for advancement through the ranks?

Details about the position you have applied for

Who does the position report to?
How long has the position been open?
Who were the previous employees in the position?
Is it a new position? If it is, why was it created?
What are the opportunities for promotion?
What happened to previous incumbents?

The company's history and future plans

When was the company established?
Does the company show steady growth over the years?
Is the company expanding its business or stagnating?
Who are the major shareholders (if the company is listed on the stock market)?

——— Preparing your résumé ———

Once you've finished your research on the employer you are interested in, you can start writing your résumé. If you have already compiled it, all you have to do is to tailor it to suit the employer and the position for which you are going to apply. Job seekers don't usually perceive modifying their résumé as a crucial step in getting an invitation to a job interview. Nothing could be further from the truth.

How do you arouse interest in a person who has never seen you or spoken to you? How do you tell employers the most important facts of your life in a matter of minutes? How do you present your achievements and outline your strengths on a couple of pages? By compiling an effective and attractive résumé. Your résumé is everything: your school record, diplomas, certificates, degrees, experience, employment history, knowledge, strengths, interests, goals and much more, all condensed into an explosive compound whose only purpose is to knock recruiters off their feet and make them want you badly.

You have probably read some of the great old masterpieces, when the only way to win a woman's heart was through romantic letters, poetry and an occasional red rose. This is exactly how you can win an employer's heart. Not by sending them red roses, but through potent and powerful words in your résumé and letter of application.

Your résumé is the most powerful selling tool at your disposal. Invest time and money in its preparation and keep it updated. Its only purpose is to secure a job interview for you.

When applying for a job, always make that extra effort and find out the name of the person you are sending your résumé and letter of application to. A title is not enough. By addressing a person by name, you break the intimacy barrier. A person's name is the most important word in their vocabulary. Everybody wants to see his/her name written and referred to. It makes them feel important and valued.

Using names, however, is not enough. Use simple and effective language, without clichés, phrases and formalities. Write the same way you would talk to that person if he/she was standing before you. Don't try to impress too much. Be brief. Avoid going into too many details and don't boost your achievements. That is done at the interview.

How to prepare your résumé – the rules of the game

1   Prepare it yourself. Don't use agencies. Do, however, use word processing software and laser printers if you have access to them. To the average employer, presentation is often more important than substance. Sad, but true.

2   Get somebody else with a good knowledge of English grammar and style to proofread it. The more times this is done, the better.

3   Ask as many relevant people as possible to give you their opinion on the content, quality and style of your résumé.

4   Use high quality stationery, preferably a cream or light-blue colour. Although white is the norm, you want your résumé to stand out. Avoid loud colours. Subtle pastels or light-blue high quality bond stands out just enough to be noticed and remembered.

5   Don't lie or exaggerate about your accomplishments. Honesty is the best policy as far as résumés are concerned (interviews are slightly different, as we will see later).

6   Use active words that project an image of a person who takes action, assumes responsibility and achieves results: designed,

calculated, established, started, initiated, introduced, managed, supervised, monitored, investigated, trained, achieved, increased, saved . . .

7 The following facts don't have a place on your résumé (make sure you leave them out): your present or past salaries; expected salary; the names of your references; a photograph of yourself; your nationality; height, weight, eye-colour, names of your spouse and children.

8 Optional information is your age, your marital status, hobbies and outside interests. I would recommend that you leave all of them out. These facts have nothing to do with your ability to do a job; they are totally irrelevant and may serve as an 'invitation' to some sort of discrimination by employers.

9 Your objective is another sticky point. Many job-hunting books say it's 'a must'. I wouldn't recommend it. However, should you decide to include it, make it brief, concise and place it at the very beginning of the résumé.

The worst résumé writers' mistakes

Too long

The information provided is not concise, relevant and captivating. It resembles a fairy tale not a direct, straight-to-the-point communication medium. There are many redundant words and information is often repeated.

Too short

There isn't sufficient data to enable employers to evaluate the candidate properly. In some cases, long employment records cannot possibly be condensed to one or two pages, which is the norm for résumés. It is perfectly acceptable to produce a longer résumé if the circumstances require such an approach.

Poor presentation

The résumé is sloppy, untidy, poorly designed (graphically) or poorly reproduced (photocopied). The paper is folded too many times and resembles a bus ticket, not a professional presentation.

Spelling and grammar errors

The first impression spelling and grammar errors create is a lack of attention to detail and concentrated effort, both of which are serious flaws in any occupation. The recruiter gets the impression that a candidate isn't very keen to create a good impression and get the job.

Too slick

It is obvious that the résumé has been prepared by a professional. It may also be boastful, and some exaggeration is suspected, seriously undermining the candidate's credibility.

This is the **right** way to do it.

STEPHANIE HABER
5 Great James Street
London, WC1N 3DA
071 938 1055 (Home)   071 975 3364 (W/H)

Personal: Born 29 September 1964

Education: BSc in accounting, University of London, 1986; MBA in Technology Management, University of London, 1992

Experience:

Feb 1992 – present

Logitech Consulting Company
Contracts officer

In charge of the Contracts Department. Responsible for the negotiation and administration of contracts, liaison with clients, tender preparation and approval. Developed a project status reporting system using networked Macintosh computers. Attended courses in Quality Control and became proficient in ISO 9000 series of quality standards.

Proficient in the use of word processing, spreadsheet, database and other PC-based software packages.

July 1989 – Jan 1992

Specialised Engineering Co.
Project controller

Responsible for the administration of projects and contracts for a toolmaking engineering company. Established internal quality control procedures for contract administration tasks. Achieved cost savings in the order of £300,000 per year.

Developed and successfully implemented a new computerised system for cost monitoring and control.

May 1986 – June 1989

Smith and Partners – Public Accountants
Graduate Trainee

Responsibilities included general accounting work, preparation of tax returns, auditing of clients' accounts and internal procedures, budget and cash flow preparations. After the initial training, appointed account supervisor for two major clients in the engineering sector.

Membership of professional bodies: Associate of the Institute of Chartered Accountants

Other interests: Computers, netball, winter sports

References: Available on request after the interview

This is the **wrong** way

STEPHANIE HABER
5 Great James Street
London, WC1N 3DA
071 938 1055 (Home)   071 975 3364 (W/H)

Objective: A well-paid administrative position with an engineering or construction company in the inner London area. Will consider short assignments outside London, but only if the salary offered is at least 20% above my present remuneration.

Personal: Born 29 September 1964; Height: 169 cm; Weight: 56 kg; Eyes: Blue; Hair: Brown; Happily married to John, no children; Health: Excellent (except an occasional migraine and allergies).

Hobbies and interests: Computers, netball, winter sports

Education:

1982–1986	BSc in accounting, University of London
1988 1992	MBA in Technology Management, University of London

Employment history:

1986– **Smith and Partners – Public Accountants**
1989 Graduate Trainee

Performed general accounting work, preparation of tax returns, and checking of clients' accounts. Also performed budget and cash flow preparations under close supervision. After the initial training, resigned and joined Specialised Engineering Company which offered higher salary and better conditions.

1989– **Specialised Engineering Co.**
1992 Project controller

Performed the administration of projects and contracts for a small toolmaking engineering company. Established basic internal quality control procedures for contract administration tasks. Participated in the development and implementation of a new computerised system for cost monitoring and control. Left because of personal differences with the Project Supervisor.

1992– **Logitech Consulting Company**
1994 Contracts officer

Hired to oversee the operation of the Contracts Department, which included negotiation and administration of contracts, liaison with clients, tender preparation and approval. Developed a project status reporting system using networked Macintosh computers. Attended courses in Quality Control. Due to company's downsizing efforts, became redundant in January 1994.

References:

Peter Seymour, Senior Partner, Smith and Partners
Alison Jones, Project Supervisor, Specialised Engineering Co.
Michael Taylor, Engineering Admin Manager, Logitech Consulting Company

Analysing the mistakes

1   The objective is demanding and shows bad taste. It lacks modesty and moderation. It creates a very bad first impression.

2   There are too many personal details. Height, weight, the colour of candidate's eyes and hair, husband's name, health details are all unnecessary. Even marital status could be omitted.

3   There is no need to specify the exact periods of study. Graduating year usually suffices.

4   On the other hand, employment experience requires months to be specified, not just years of employment. 1986–1989 could mean January 1986 until December 1989, which is almost four years, or December 1986 until January 1989, which is just over two years! This is a very common trick used by job hoppers and is despised by employers.

5   Employment history doesn't sound very nice, it refers to past tense. 'Employment achievements' 'experience', or simply 'employment' is much better.

6   Employment details are always listed in the reverse chronological order, starting with the most current position and ending with the first job a candidate held.

7   It isn't necessary to list the references on your résumé. It takes valuable space that could be better used for other purposes, such as listing your achievements and accomplishments.

8   The reasons for leaving should not be found on a résumé. It is much wiser to discuss them at a job interview (only if asked by the interviewer). That way you can explain exactly what happened, how and why. If simply stated on a résumé, certain facts (personal differences, retrenchments, etc) will certainly create negative impressions.

—— Writing letters of application ——

There are some general rules you should follow when applying for a job and writing letters of application. If you follow them, you may find yourself in a new job sooner than you think. This doesn't mean that you have to follow the rules to get a job blindly. It only means that if you do get a job without doing your homework properly, you got it not because of your efforts, but despite them.

Rule 1: Research and investigation

When applying for a job that was advertised in the press, before writing your letter of application, study the advert in depth. Analyse the words, the order of sentences, the syntax. Try to read between the lines and get a feeling about the person who wrote the advert and the company's way of thinking. What personal and professional characteristics are important to the employer? What type of person are they looking for? What are the minimum requirements (absolute musts) where qualifications and experience are concerned? What are the 'nice to have' attributes? Where do you fit in that description? Which of your strong points could you emphasise in your application?

Only when you have answered all these questions, may you say 'I've done my homework properly, let's get into writing the application that's going to win me a job interview.' Notice the word 'win'. Your application has to be a winning application, your résumé a winning résumé. Writing letters of application is like painting. The longest, most tedious and monotonous task is information gathering and research. It can be likened to preparation: cleaning, sanding, filling, sanding, cleaning, priming. Then comes the painting, the brush strokes. The compilation of your résumé and letter of application is possibly the easiest and quickest task of them all.

Rule 2: Language and style

Your letter of application and résumé serve one purpose only: to get you invited for a job interview. They are your only presentation tools beforehand, so make sure you use them properly. Avoid phrases and clichés in your letter. Your language should be alive and vivid and should attract the reader's attention. Spelling mistakes and grammatical or syntax errors are cardinal sins and will almost certainly cause your application to end up in the waste-paper basket.

It helps immensely to have somebody who can proofread your application documents and give you an honest and unbiased feedback on the quality, clarity and style of your writing. Two pairs of eyes see more than one, so don't hesitate to show your draft letters to people who are willing to help.

Rule 3: Presentation

Give your letter of application and your résumé a nice look. Use only top quality paper. Print it out on a laser printer or a good quality dot-matrix. Be conservative in your use of colours. Black or dark blue for text and white or light pastel colours for paper are the best to stick to. Use fonts that are easy to read. Avoid fancy fonts and try not to use more than two styles: one for headings, one for paragraphs. Do, however, use italics and bold fonts for the facts and achievements that need emphasising.

The question of aesthetics: when you mail your résumé, don't fold it or staple the pages together. Send it with your letter of application in an A4 size envelope. This projects a true professional image. An application folded two or three times looks just like a piece of junk mail and usually ends up in the same place – the waste-paper basket.

> *Three things are of paramount importance for creating a great résumé: presentation, presentation and presentation.*

Before you seal the envelope, just make sure two things are not missing: your signature and a copy of your résumé. You would be surprised how many times applicants forget to do these simple things.

Rule 4: The follow-up

When you send your job application to a prospective employer, make a note in your diary and keep photocopies of all correspondence. This is especially important if you have more than one version of your résumé, tailored to suit each particular application. That way you won't be caught unprepared at the interview should the interviewer, based on the information supplied on your résumé, ask you some specific question or need clarification of a particular situation.

After a week or so, telephone the employer just to confirm that they have received your application. Don't leave anything to chance. Display initiative. Find out how long the short-listing of applicants is going to take, so you can prepare yourself for the interview, should you be on the short list. Make a plan for your interview preparations and stick to it.

The biggest mistake you can make in job hunting is not to follow up your application. Always remind employers of your candidacy and project keen interest in the progress of your application. Most employers will appreciate your resourcefulness and systematic, organised approach to career issues.

This **is** how to do it:

STEPHANIE HABER,
5 Great James Street
London, WC1N 3DA
071 938 1055 (Home)   071 975 3364 (W/H)

13 February 1994

Mr Nigel Pettigrove
Personnel Manager
Booth, Smith and Partners
29 Abingdon Road
London W8 6AL

Dear Mr Pettigrove

With reference to your advertisement in *The Times* on 28 January 1994, I would like to express my strong interest in the position of Senior Contract Administrator.

After seven years in various administrative positions in the consulting sector, I am ready for new challenges. I am sure my education, theoretical and practical knowledge and experience in project management, negotiation and administration of contracts will benefit your engineering consultancy.

My strong analytical and technical skills, and the ability to work with people, and on urgent and demanding tasks, should enable me to start achieving results in the shortest possible time. I have had experience in liaison with clients, vendors and Government and statutory bodies, in budget preparations, cost control, supervision of office personnel, coordinating, planning and report writing and presentation.

The current economic climate requires an innovative and rational approach to project management and engineering in general. I understand all aspects of client service, reliability and safety aspects of engineering, as well as the implementation of Total Quality Control methods. Most of all, I understand people and how to work with them in a result-orientated team environment.

A copy of my résumé and qualifications is enclosed for your reference. Should you require further information do not hesitate to contact me at any time. I would welcome the opportunity to meet with you to discuss this position and my background in more detail, and to explore the ways I could contribute to the ongoing success of your firm.

I appreciate your consideration and look forward to hearing from you.

Yours sincerely,

Stephanie Haber

Stephanie Haber

Encl.

This is **not** how to do it:

STEPHANIE HABER
5 Great James Street
London, WC1N 3DA
071 938 1055 (Home)   071 975 3364 (W/H)

13 February 1994

Personnel Manager
Booth, Smith and Partners
29 Abingdon Road
London W8 6AL

Dear Sir

I am reading with great interest your advertisement in *The Times*. I would like to apply for the job of Senior Contract Administrator. I have been working on similar jobs for more than seven years now, so joining a prosperous company such as yours would be a nice change.

Although my background is not in engineering, I am sure I could handle the task outlined in your advertisement without major hassles. Being a Libran, my pleasant personality and popularity in the office would more than compensate for my lack of engineering qualifications.

I am looking for a challenging position with a major consulting firm in the engineering or construction sector, which doesn't involve travel and regular overtime work. I just got married and am planning to have my first child soon. I would consider relocating, should an attractive package be offered, especially the health insurance coverage.

Currently I am unemployed and have been using this time to learn French and improve my career prospects.

I have enclosed a copy of my résumé and qualifications. If you require further information do not hesitate to contact me at any time. If you think my qualifications and experience would be suitable for this opening, I would be glad to attend an interview.

Thank you for your time.

Yours sincerely,

Stephanie Haber

Stephanie Haber

Encl.

Analysing the mistakes

1   The second letter is addressed to the Personnel Manager. It is much better to address it to the actual person and to avoid 'Dear Sir' or 'Dear Sirs' salutation. Everyone likes to see his or her name on a letter and it's much easier to create a friendly and intimate feeling when addressing a person by name.

2   Almost every sentence begins with 'I . . .'. Avoid this as much as you can. A letter of application should tell the employer what you could do for them, not what you want for yourself! Statements such as 'I am reading with great interest . . .' or 'I would like . . .' put people off and should not be used.

3   The fact that you are currently unemployed should be omitted and the reason should be explained at the interview (only if you are asked to do so).

4   The second paragraph emphasises the lack of engineering qualifications and tries to compensate for that by mentioning the applicant's star sign and personality traits. It would be funny if it wasn't tragic.

5   The third paragraph projects a picture of someone who cares only about her spare time, her family life and the employment benefits. If I was a personnel manager reading this letter, I wouldn't go past this point. The lights would go off, the curtain would come down. This is a typical 'waste-paper basket' case.

6   The ending paragraph is doubtful. The applicant herself isn't sure that her qualification and experience are adequate for the job. She leaves it to the personnel manager to decide if that is the case, instead of charging ahead with self-confidence and proclaiming 'I would welcome the opportunity to explore the ways I could help your firm in its ongoing success . . .'. What a world of difference!

7   A letter addressed 'Dear Sir' or 'Dear Sirs' should never end with 'Yours sincerely'. 'Yours faithfully' is the correct wording to be used.

2

WHAT CAN YOU OFFER?

— Personal audit (your +/− sheet) —

To know where you are going and how to get there, you must first know yourself.

Vincent Clement Stone, *The Success System That Never Fails*

People have a surprising tendency towards self-deception. They usually overestimate their strengths and underestimate their weaknesses. They concentrate on successful dealings with others, but forget how to deal properly with themselves. Being smart and astute when dealing with others does not necessarily mean that you are not fooling yourself.

On the other hand, underestimating your strengths and/or overestimating your weaknesses is even worse; that sort of attitude certainly won't help you in job hunting. As always in life, balance should be reached.

Self-knowledge is the key: whether you design skyscrapers or run the lunch counter, you cannot use your talents to their fullest unless you also know your weaknesses.

Mark H. McCormack, *The 110% Solution*

Job hunters' personalities

Professional psychologists like classifying people. This helps them make general assumptions about our habits, personalities, attitudes and behaviour. For illustrative purposes I'll do something similar here. We'll take a look at some typical personalities and their approach to job hunting and interviewing. You may recognise some of your own attributes here. That is the main aim of this exercise – to start you thinking about your own personality, your own good and bad points.

The straight shooters Owing to their inherent honesty and high integrity, straight shooters always tell the truth and nothing but the truth to interviewers. They don't know how to emphasise their good points and minimise their weaknesses. More often than not they are losers in the job game.

The professionals Professionals do everything right, from preparing for the interview to the 'Thank you' note afterwards. They know what employers want to hear. They are winners in the job game. Hopefully, after reading this book and with some practice, you will become a professional, too.

The con artists Con artists hardly possess any relevant qualifications or skills for the jobs they apply for, but being masters of interviewing and manipulating people, they are offered jobs quite easily.

The epicureans Epicureans enjoy life to the fullest. They 'work to live' and don't care for overtime and commitment to the company they work for. Not particularly ambitious.

The workaholics Opposite to the epicureans. All work and no play makes them dull boys and girls. They sacrifice everything for work. Of course, the employers love them.

The Machiavellians Machiavellians' credo is: 'The end justifies the means'. They could be either professionals or con artists. The other types seldom adopt this philosophy. The Machiavellians are high achievers, and while they strive to win, they sometimes use and abuse everything and everybody that can help them to get to the top.

Your task at the interview is to convince the potential employer that you are somewhere between a straight shooter and a workaholic. However, the purpose of this book is to help you become the professional interviewee, no matter which group you belong to, and whatever your philosophy in life is.

Self-evaluation sheets and how to use them

On the following pages you can find examples of basic self-assessment sheets. Copy them, then write a short evaluation of each particular strength or weakness, as it applies to you. Use short statements like **OK**, if you are satisfied with a particular skill, **to improve** if you feel the need and room for improvement in that area, or **very strong** if you have some outstanding skill. For example:

Willing to learn	through courses, on the job – OK
Management skills	supervisory experience, management courses
Experience	two years in accounting, good start
Able to work under pressure	yes, on urgent tasks – OK
Takes initiative	occasionally, not too often – to improve
	or
Language skills	good language skills – very strong
Self-esteem	generally good, sometimes low – to improve
Now work experience	limited experience, two years
Low grades in school/ university	good grades – OK
Bad references	nothing detrimental – OK

You can create your own sheets if you find the enclosed ones not suitable, or add your own strengths and weaknesses at the bottom of the sheets. Whatever you do, be honest with yourself. Nobody else will see your self-assessment. Keep your sheets in a safe place. As you make progress and improve your skills and/or eliminate your weaknesses, you can change them or fill in new ones.

After the self-evaluation sheets, you'll find an example of a work experience analysis sheet. To prepare yourself for an interview, use the copies of the sheet to analyse your past performance. Use a separate sheet for each major task or project you have done, or for a group of smaller interrelated jobs. By doing this evaluation properly, you will make it much easier for yourself later when you prepare your own answers to typical interview questions in Chapter 6.

Again, you can customise the sheet to suit your preferences, or create your own. In this case, form is not important, the essence is.

Before you start analysing your past experiences and filling in your sheets, read Chapter 6 to get a basic idea about:

- the areas interviewers are interested in;
- typical interview questions;
- the reasons interviewers ask those questions;
- model answers, which should be a starting point for your own customised answers.

When analysing and classifying your past tasks, experiences and achievements, try to group and evaluate them on the basis of critical factors such as initiative, integrity, ability to learn, adaptability, planning and control, attention to detail, work standards, etc. The questions in Chapter 6 are based on those dimensions. Your self-analysis should help you to come up with examples that illustrate each of those dimensions. For example, some of the more important cases would be:

- when you achieved more than you expected;
- when you failed despite giving your best;
- when you succeeded because you persisted for a period of time;
- when you successfully implemented someone else's idea;
- when you successfully implemented your own idea;
- when you made a difficult decision;
- when you did more than was required;
- when you failed/succeeded because of poor/proper planning;
- when you felt you could have done a better job;
- when you had to go against the rules or policies in order to get a job done or achieve the planned target.

When you finish your objective analysis (be honest with yourself), identify your mistakes and areas for improvement. The last step will be to find a way of emphasising the things you have done right, covering up the things that went wrong and therefore lessening the impact your mistakes may have on the interviewers.

> *Even if it's true, never confess that you did something selfish, silly, foolish, unlawful, unsafe, or that you acted irresponsibly, impulsively, or against the rules. Absolute honesty and frankness are precious commodities, except in a job interview.*

SELF-EVALUATION SHEET 1

My strengths and assets:

Independent or team player

Self-starter

Good communication skills

Willing to learn

Management skills

Experience

Able to work under pressure

Takes initiative

Reliable and responsible

Flexible

Cooperative/easy to work with

Persistent

Decisive

Able to delegate

Thorough (attention to details)

Innovative

Loyal

This page is photocopiable

SELF-EVALUATION SHEET 2

My weaknesses and handicaps:

Poor English

Low self-esteem

No work experience

Low grades in school/at university

Bad references from previous employers

Immigrant or member of ethnic minority

Physical or mental handicap

Not enough education

Poor communication skills

Poor interviewing skills

Unsystematic and inefficient

Too specialised

Too much of a generalist

Tendency to procrastinate

Lack of drive/ambition

Lack of planning

Lack of self-discipline

Poor health

This page is photocopiable

WORK EXPERIENCE ANALYSIS SHEET

Employer:

Date:

Case:

Situation:

My task:

The outcome (results):

Accomplishments:

Mistakes made:

The cause of those mistakes:

Lessons learned:

This page is photocopiable

__ Eliminating your weaknesses and __ neutralising other obstacles

At the job interview, the employer will try to find out details, not only about your achievements, knowledge and strong points, but also about your shortcomings, inconsistencies and weaknesses. Your first task before the interview is to discover what your flaws are and then either to improve them and transform them into strengths, or conceal them by emphasising your strengths (something like 'Attack is the best form of defence' tactic).

Whenever you have to tell the interviewer about mistakes you have made (keep it to the minimum) quickly point out what you've learned from those lessons and stress that you never repeat your mistakes. That is the best way to neutralise the negative impact your past mistakes may have.

Ideally, you should try the proper way: forcing yourself to change for the better. To be successful in that approach, two things are required: first, it takes an awful lot of time and second, it demands determination, perseverance and hard, hard work. Most job applicants have neither of these.

Should you be brave and opt for a radical change of your shortcomings, start by visiting your local library and studying the numerous self-help and self-improvement books available, or by enrolling on motivation and 'self-mastery' courses. Obstacles belong in the same category as weaknesses. Both are working against you. These are some of the significant hindrances that you should eliminate, neutralise or reduce.

Inferiority complex

> *I have no inferiority complex, and I'm not frightened by big-sounding names. When I'm confronted by powerful people, I remind myself that all men use lavatory paper.*
>
> Robert Maxwell

No additional words are necessary here. In a nutshell, don't be afraid of anybody, don't overestimate anybody and don't be intimidated by anybody. Maintain your self-esteem and never lose belief in your abilities. Be constantly aware of your value. You can even inflate it a bit, just don't underestimate yourself and doubt your position.

Balance of power

> *The price of ability does not depend on merit, but on supply and demand.*
>
> George Bernard Shaw, 'Socialism And Superior Brains' in *Fortnightly Review*, April 1894

Most job hunters these days feel that employers dictate terms in the recession-hit job market, due to increased competition for jobs and the influx of high calibre applicants who are prepared to work for little reward. That statement is only partially true.

By using the right strategies, a planned and systematic approach to interviewing, and by utilising all leverage and help at your disposal, you can greatly diminish the negative aspects of the tight job market. Employers do want the best applicants, and are usually prepared to stretch themselves to get them.

The majority, (say 80 per cent), of people who apply for the job you want will not pass the first, résumé, stage. They have no chance whatsoever. Out of the other twenty per cent who are qualified and have the right experience, a short list will be created. Your first task is to be on that list. To achieve that you need a good résumé. The remaining tasks are covered in this book.

Competitors

Never underestimate the quality and strength of your competitors. Always prepare yourself thoroughly for the interview. Explore all possibilities, especially things that can go wrong, because there is a great chance that they will. Keep in mind that job hunting, especially interviewing, is pure Darwinism: only the fittest candidate will survive and get the job. However, to overestimate your competition would be an even worse sin. By doing that you automatically lower your self-esteem and your chances for success.

In a nutshell, be confident and composed. Don't compare yourself with others. Compete with yourself. Strive towards constant improvement of your skills and abilities, especially communication techniques and job-interviewing skills.

> *While competing for jobs, we all make mistakes.*
> *Your goal should just be to make fewer mistakes*
> *than your opponents.*

Improving your interviewing skills and performance

One thing job hunters have to understand is that their skills are commodities that are sought after by employers. Skills on the job market could be equated to other commodities on the stock market. Their values go up or down, depending on the supply and demand, i.e. how many people are buying or selling the shares (looking for a job) and at what price (how much money they are prepared to accept in return for their services).

Your ongoing task is to keep improving your skills and 'adding value' to them. By skills I mean your professional knowledge and know-how as well as your job-hunting skills (résumé writing, interviewing, career planning). Your job-hunting skills are not valuable to employers, but as a selling and marketing tool they are extremely valuable to you, because they help you to promote your real abilities, knowledge and experience.

Interviewing skills are probably the most important in the whole process, and, unfortunately, the most difficult to master. The good news is that these skills are portable – you can apply them in any real life situation and reap the benefits. We are not talking about God-given skills and abilities. We are talking about common-sense: talking to other people, listening to them, interacting with them. We are talking about fundamental techniques in handling people.

In real life, most of the time we don't see or feel the direct consequences when we use (or don't use) our people-handling skills. In the job interview things are more obvious. There are only two possible outcomes – you either got the job or you didn't. It is much easier to measure your performance against the known standards and expectations. The aim of this book is to explain and analyse these standards and to advise you on the best tactics at your disposal, and when and how to use them.

The next step is to go through a few of the basic interviewing skills and ways of improving them.

Learn how to listen

Most people are not good listeners. They never listen to anyone for long. They talk mostly about themselves and interrupt others without waiting for them to finish talking. Even if they don't interrupt, they don't pay attention to what others are saying, because they are busy rehearsing what they are going to say next. That is probably even worse than talking too much, for they are neither making a point, nor hearing one.

These are all cardinal sins in the job interview. You should listen very carefully, not only to what the interviewers are saying, but how they are saying it. It is not enough simply to hear, you have to listen aggressively. Listening skills are among the most valuable possessions you may have.

Remember the following rules:

- Do not jump to conclusions before the interviewer finishes the statement.
- Never, ever, interrupt the interviewer, even if you strongly disagree with him/her.
- Do not discard the information that you don't want to hear or that you don't like.
- Listen for main ideas, not for details.
- If the interviewer talks slowly, don't let your mind wander. No daydreaming. Use that time to analyse what is being said and why, to anticipate, weigh the evidence, mentally rehearse the interviewer's points and listen 'between the lines' for clues.
- Don't tune out if the delivery is poor. Concentrate on content, not on errors in speech.
- Fight or avoid distractions. Concentrate.

Be time-sensitive

The main problem in interviewing is time. The interviewer has to evaluate all aspects of the candidate in a strictly limited amount of time, say an hour or so. On the other hand, you have to convince the interviewer that you are the best person for the job and you have only one hour (or less) to do so. Therefore, you both have to be time-sensitive.

Experienced interviewers know or feel how much time they can, or want, to spend on each particular question or area to be covered. You should know too, to the best of your abilities. The time control is usually in your hands, owing to the fact that to answer the interviewer's questions takes much more time than to ask them. Knowing that, you must constantly read the interviewer and make sure that you confine yourself within certain time limits.

Your answers should be neither too short nor too long. By giving very short answers you force the interviewer to ask you additional questions and the fluidity of the whole conversation is gone. There are too many pauses and the whole interview sounds like interrogation. On the other hand, if your answers are too long, the interviewer may get all sorts of ideas:

- the candidate is not capable of distinguishing between important and unimportant information;
- he/she has got no respect for me and my time;
- he/she bores me immensely;
- he/she would not be able to keep secrets and confidential information to himself/herself, therefore could not be trusted.

Once the interview starts, you must have a clear idea of how much time to devote to each answer and when to ask relevant questions. Of course, don't be rigid. Just remember the old cliché: 'time is money'. It's certainly true at the job interview.

Improve your vocabulary

Your ability to communicate, especially through the spoken word, is exceptionally important! Words are very powerful; used wisely, they will help you go a long way towards the top.

With words you can relate to people and communicate your feelings and thoughts to them. Therefore, words are the best tool for influencing and controlling people!

Your vocabulary is you – it's your fingerprint. So, if you want to improve your image and your chances for success, make sure you continually expand your vocabulary. Research shows that only three to four thousand words separate people with large vocabularies from those with small ones.

The way we say things is quite often more important than what we actually say!

In contrast to learning the grammatical rules and the syntax of English language, vocabulary expanding can be fun. You can do it 'formally', by studying text-books and encyclopedias, or 'informally', by jotting down every unknown word you encounter while reading a book, a magazine or even while watching television.

Later, go through a good dictionary to find the exact meaning of the words and try to remember the contexts in which they were used.

The fact is that the vocabulary of an average person almost stops growing when they reach the mid-twenties. Therefore, it is necessary to make this extra effort and start building up your knowledge of words.

3

— SELLING YOURSELF —

Everyone lives by selling something.

Robert Louis Stevenson

- **Your appearance: dress for the part** -

Job hunting is like a game: when you write your résumé and apply for a job, you're in the qualification rounds. Should you pass the qualifications you get a place in the final game: the job interview.

It isn't difficult to be a winner on a paper. But in real life situations, the differences will stand out, and your looks and appearance will contribute to those differences.

The authors of some self-improvement books I've read devoted ten or twenty pages to the ways of 'dressing for success'. With all due respect, I find it ridiculous. Individual styles are different, fashion changes every year or so, people in various countries dress differently, the positions you will be interviewed for will dictate different norms and standards, different employers place different values on the way you may dress.

Some common-sense rules do exist, though. Let's take a look at them:

1   Always be clean and well groomed. Pay special attention to your hair, nails and teeth. They should be spotless!

2   Never wear too much jewellery, especially big rings, brace-lets, cuff links or golden chains, emphasising the macho-image. Earrings for men are definitely not recommended.

3   Don't wear short-sleeved shirts at the interview. You don't want to look like a used car salesperson or a campaigning politician (unless you are one).

4   Never take off your suit jacket, unless you have to. The jacket gives you more authority.

5   Depending on the job you are applying for, carry a good briefcase, preferably black leather. It will enhance your image tremendously. This particularly applies to accountants, law-yers, engineers, managers and other professionals.

6   Always wear a wrist-watch. It will help you project a business image and discreetly tell the interviewer that your time is also valuable. A word of caution here – don't look at the watch. This is a mortal sin. It tells the interviewer that you are anxious to get out and that you aren't really interested in the job.

7   Men should wear an expensive, silk tie of appropriate pattern. Since most men's suits look alike, a nice tie contributes to your image much more than you would expect. Stick to conserva-tive designs with a dash of originality. Bow-ties or Texan leather ties are not recommended (except for waiters and oil magnates).

Dress so that you feel you look good.

Never follow the trends if they don't suit you. Some 'consultants' say: dress in black or dark blue only. That's nonsense. You may not look good wearing dark colours if your complexion is fair. Follow your own feelings or consult your spouse or a good friend. Unbiased advice is always welcome.

If you need a new outfit, new suit or dress, invest your money wisely. Buy first-class only. It will be money well spent. If you want to give a first-class performance, don't go wearing second-class attire.

It is advisable to have at least two different outfits, just in case something goes wrong. Besides, if you go for a second or third interview with the same employer, you should change your clothes, otherwise you may project a picture of a typical job-beggar: one suit, timidity, lack of originality, stiffness, predictability.

Don't keep your interview outfits 'for interviews only'. Wear them when you go out to restaurants or the theatre. That will make you feel comfortable wearing them and help you to be relaxed and natural at the interview.

——— Talking about yourself ———

Man is like a rabbit, you catch him by the ears.

Blaise Pascal

Your purpose in a job interview is to convince the prospective employer that you are the most suitable candidate for the job, even if you are not.

Your success in interviewing will be determined more by your ability to market and promote yourself than by your actual knowledge and work experience.

In order to do that, you have to present yourself to the interviewers in the right way, tell them what you have done in the past and what you could do for them in the future, should they select you for the job. The bottom line is therefore a simple one. How to achieve it is another story.

Some people find talking about themselves difficult and feel uncomfortable while doing so. If you want to become a 'professional interviewee', learn to talk about yourself in the most effective manner, without false modesty, but without boasting, either.

There are some basic rules for your 'self-presentation'. Study them carefully and constantly keep them on your mind. The effort will pay off, believe me. Here they are:

1   Say only good things about your previous employers.

2   Be future-orientated or, at least, leave an impression that you are!

3   Select your words carefully.

4   Avoid inappropriate questions.

5   Listen carefully to what the interviewers say and frame your answers accordingly.

6   Some interviewers like to talk about themselves. Let them.

7   Develop and use your own style to deliver a perfect performance.

8   Never argue with the interviewers.

9   Always talk in other person's terms.

10   Be prepared to talk about your mistakes and shortcomings.

11   Place a high value on yourself – don't be a 'job-beggar'.

Let's take a look at each of them in turn.

Say only good things about your previous employers

Even if your boss treated you unfairly, if you didn't like your former place of work and the people you worked with, keep it to yourself. Do not criticise, complain or accuse. Think about some positive things you can say about your former employers and remember to project sincerity, even when 'bending the truth', for you'll be bending it in your favour!

Let me tell you a story about a personnel officer interviewing applicants for a supervisory position on the shop floor.

After the initial interviews he selected the two best candidates for the final interview. After talking to the first man, the personnel officer had no further questions for the candidate. At the end of the interview, the candidate asked the following question: 'What could you tell me about the people who work here? What are the workers like?'

The personnel man wasn't sure what to say and responded with a question: 'What were the people like at your last place of work?'

The applicant looked at the personnel officer and said: 'The company I just left had mainly pretty bad people. They were not friendly and I wasn't happy there. The management had no respect for workers, who were difficult to supervise. They were just no good. That is why I want to join your company.'

The interviewer looked directly at the candidate and said, 'Well, I'm afraid that most people we employ here are of the same kind. Things you are looking for are not easy to find.'

After interviewing the second candidate and answering similar questions about the job itself and the company's plans for the future, the personnel officer asked the interviewee: 'Tell me something about the people you used to work with and the workers you used to supervise'.

'The people at my former place of work were really nice and friendly. I haven't had any problems supervising the shop floor. I enjoyed the time I spent with them, but due to the limited opportunities there for myself and my family I am looking for a position with the company like yours. It was not easy to leave, but we had no choice.'

'Well, you are in luck, young man', the interviewer said, 'because that's exactly the kind of people that work for this company. You'll really like them and they'll like you. Welcome aboard!'

We find exactly what we seek.

Be future-orientated (or at least, leave an impression that you are)

Most applicants think that prospective employers are interested in their past. They are, but only because they believe that by analysing the candidate's past, they can predict his/her future behaviour and performance.

Whatever you say about your education and past experience, say it in such a way as to convince the interviewers that:

— **57** —

- you were in control of events;
- you achieved something in those particular situations;
- you can do the same good job for them.

By being a future-orientated person you project a sense of purpose and direction. Employers like that attitude and place a high value on it.

Select your words carefully

In order to create an image of competency, efficiency and integrity in the interviewer's eyes, use words that are easy to understand, short and expressive, words that generate the right mental pictures and are appropriate. By using wrong, inappropriate or confusing words, you may make the interviewer think that you:

- are boring and dull;
- are full of yourself and will have difficulty in working with others;
- don't really understand what you are talking about;
- talk in terms that are too general and cannot give examples of real life situations.

The bottom line in choosing the words is to keep the interviewer's attention!

Avoid inappropriate questions

Victor Kiam, one of the most successful entrepreneurs, tells the following story in his book *Going For It!*:

> *If you are in position where you are trying to secure a position, you certainly don't want the company to think you are already dreaming about retirement. Not too long ago, a young man ended an interview by asking me what Remington's pension plan was. He was about 25 years old! I answered him, 'Son, you'll never find out'.*

Always keep in mind that just one clumsy question may set you back or even get you out of the game completely. If you are unsure about the impact that the question you intend to ask will have on the interviewer, don't ask it. But, if there is nothing to lose and a lot to gain, go for it. The real challenge is to assess the current situation and make that decision in a matter of seconds.

This is where interviewing experience and know-how come into the equation. But since interviewing is not mathematics, my advice to you would be to rely on your own gut feelings.

Listen carefully to what the interviewers say and frame your answers accordingly

Say, for example, the interviewer tells you at the beginning of the interview that the position requires someone energetic, hard-working and committed. Further down the line you should use this priceless information to frame your answers.

For example, if asked 'What were the reasons for your success on that project?' you may answer: 'I worked long hours and committed myself to the project. It required lots of energy, but I always give one hundred per cent.' The interviewer will think: 'This is the type of person I want for this job.'

This type of feedback will prove the most useful in interviewing.

Some interviewers like to talk about themselves. Let them.

A few years ago I was interviewed for an engineering position with one of Australia's largest companies. The Chief Engineer was a friendly guy, I felt at ease with him and the interview went on well. It was probably the easiest one in my whole career! Why? Because the interviewer talked all the time. I hardly spoke a word.

He explained the job to me, the company's history and plans, career opportunities and so on. Did I interrupt him? You can bet I didn't. After about an hour or so in his office we parted on very friendly terms. A week after that I was invited again to his office where he introduced me to my future boss. The same scenario took place again. I was offered a job almost without effort. God certainly works in mysterious ways.

Develop and use your own style to deliver a perfect performance

The style is the man.

Robert Frost

It isn't easy to define style, but people remember style as much as substance. In the job game, style should be recognised as an important factor in dramatising your ideas, getting your message across to the interviewers and making the right impressions on them.

Style is closely related to your personality and your socio-economic class. Style can be observed through the way you walk, talk, through your vocabulary, your sense of humour, your manners, clothes, your smile and gestures.

It is not easy to change your style, however it is not impossible. It takes practice and self-control. There are a number of self-improvement books that deal with this. Study them. There is nothing to lose, and a lot to gain. The rest is up to you.

Never argue with the interviewer

Keep your ego from ruining your chances of success: Never argue or question the interviewer's views!

I remember some of my colleagues in college, not because we were friends or because they were smart, but because they used to argue with the lecturers and professors, who in turn grew to dislike them. They eventually passed the exams, but with much greater difficulties than the rest of us. The other side used every opportunity for vindication.

There is no retaliation of this kind in interviewing, but you can be sure that you won't get the job. Period. By strongly expressing your views and criticising or questioning the interviewer you may exhilarate your spirit and feel good for a moment, but you are going to lose in the long run.

Always talk in other person's terms

Each one of us could talk about ourselves for hours and hours, because we are our own favourite subject. But the interviewers are not interested in you directly, all they want to know is:

- Are you qualified to do the job?
- Can you do the job?
- Will you do the job?

So, the purpose of the interview is to say as much as possible about ourselves in an organised and logical manner, therefore convincing the person across the table that we can do the job better than other candidates. To get your message across always try to establish what it is that the interviewer wants – what sort of person would he like to see in that job, what traits does he like or dislike in people, what factors does he consider important in successful performance in the job, and so on.

Always talk in terms of the interviewer's interests.

The principle above applies to any kind of human relationship, not just to job interviews. Here is a little story that I would like you to remember whenever you talk to other people:

An older lady and her nephew went to buy her a car. The first car salesman asked the lady: 'What type of car do you have in mind, madam?'

'Oh, I want a car that can take me to the library a few times a week,' the lady replied.

'Any of these cars can take you to the library,' the salesman answered. They had a look around, but left without buying a car.

In the second dealership she was asked a similar question: 'What type of car would you like?'

'I need a car which I can drive to the library a few times a week.'

'This is completely irrelevant,' the salesman said, 'you should be concerned about space, economy, quality and spare parts and service.' They again looked around, but didn't find anything of interest.

In the third dealership the lady said: 'I need a car that can take me to the library.'

'I see,' said the sales manager, 'I believe you are looking for a short-distance car for daytime driving?'

'That's exactly what I'm looking for,' the lady replied.

'Sounds like you need a small, compact car that's very easy to park and drive.'

'Spot on,' said the lady.

'I'm not sure we have got anything like that,' the manager said, 'but I'll check right now.'

After five minutes, he returned with a smile: 'We have a car for you, madam. Would you like to test-drive it?'

The lady drove the car around the block and fifteen minutes later, after signing the papers, happily drove away to the library.

Be prepared to talk about your mistakes and shortcomings

To err is human. To forgive is not company policy.

Anonymous sign to company executives

For quite a long time I was convinced that employers only wanted to know about my achievements, capabilities and successfully accomplished tasks. When you have only a limited amount of time to impress the interviewers, it is normal to give your best shot and tell them about your strengths and all nice things you could do for them. The truth, however, was slightly different. They also wanted to know about the mistakes I made, the tasks and projects I could have done better, the areas I wanted to improve in.

So, when asked about some of the mistakes you have made, you must select the least detrimental information and present it to them in such a way that the outcomes say something positive about you. The interviewers should be left with the impression that you are not repeating mistakes and that you give your best in every situation, especially when dealing with people.

The biggest mistake you can make in the interview is to imply that you have never made a mistake. Why is that so?

Employers want to hire people who have had wins and losses. That experience gives those candidates the strength and knowledge of how to capitalise on their losses and the ability to do a better job the next time by not repeating the same mistakes.

People who never make mistakes and haven't had to overcome barriers, will fall on their face when they hit the first obstacle. Employers don't like to pay for your mistakes and are not prepared to finance your 'education'. They prefer people whose former employers paid for the mistakes they made.

If you appear to discuss the events that went wrong openly, when you made a mistake or were not able to do things properly, the interviewers will be much more inclined to believe you about your accomplishments and other good points. It will help you to establish confidentiality and trust in your relationship with the interviewers and to reinforce your credibility. However, don't be a straight shooter and tell them the truth, absolute truth and nothing but the truth. Truth is a very relative term and should be treated as such. Never volunteer any information that makes you look stupid, careless, incompetent or inexperienced.

Place a high value on yourself – don't be a 'job-beggar'

*Always make yourself essential, that's been my golden
rule.*

Sir Joh Bjelke-Petersen

The biggest mistakes I made in my early days of job hunting were:

- Approaching the employers as a 'beggar' not a 'chooser'. I waited for the companies to select me and offer me a job, instead of choosing the company I wanted to work for. I left to chance most of the things I could have had control of.
- I was too timid and complacent in the whole process. I just accepted the terms, without negotiating for even one second. I accepted the salary, the benefits, the job description, etc. I even took the jobs without seeing the towns I was going to live in, without visiting my future place of work, without talking to my new colleagues. And guess what? I made the same mistake twice. Shame on me.
- When offered a job I felt that the employers were doing me a big favour. I didn't think about my assets, such as knowledge, skills and my personality. I didn't regard them as valuable commodities that the employers would benefit from. Somehow I forgot five years of hard study, sixteen years of schooling and all my past efforts. I sowed, but I didn't reap.
- I was selling my abilities short. I had a self-destructive tendency to exaggerate other people's intelligence and skills while underestimating my own. Not only that. I didn't believe in my success. I was a sceptic.

My advice to you is to do just the opposite of everything I did. Believe me, it will spare you from disappointment, frustration and self-hatred.

Never, ever, accept what's offered to you initially. Negotiate. Name your terms. Make them work hard to get you. You'll probably catch them unprepared, because too many people are beggars, not choosers. By placing a high value on yourself you automatically change your status in the employer's eyes.

Play hard to get and (later) hard to keep.

The delivery

Albert Mehrabian, an American psychologist, tried to measure the relative importance of the three basic communication channels – content, tone of voice and body language (gestures, posture, facial expressions). His research revealed that the actual content, or the words used to convey a message, contributed around ten per cent to the overall impact, compared with almost forty per cent from the tone of voice and more than fifty per cent from the body language!

Sounds illogical and hard to believe, but we have to realise that most of our thoughts and actions are based on feelings and impressions, not on logic, no matter how hard we try to project the image of systematic, no-nonsense thinkers. Every interviewer probably tries to be objective and neutral, but, at the end of the interview, his or her overall impression of you will either get you that job, or leave you unemployed. So, whatever you say, make sure that your tone of voice and your body language are reinforcing your message, not contradicting its content; otherwise, your message just won't get through to the interviewer! Keep the following proportions in your mind:

Words (message content)	10% of impact
Tone of voice	40% of impact
Body language	50% of impact

The importance of silence

Silence in a job interview can be either your powerful ally or your worst enemy. When you talk to the interviewer or answer his questions, use pauses to emphasise your point and to build up eager anticipation for what you are going to say next. Those periods of silence will give you an opportunity to make eye contact with the interviewer and study his reactions to what you've just said. Don't hesitate to use silence. Speak in a slow, relaxed manner. Pause every now and then to grab the interviewer's attention.

Some interviewers use silence as a tool for eliciting further response from a candidate. Once you say what you wanted to say, they will leave you 'in limbo' for a few, very long seconds. You must resist the urge to say something just to break the silence. Usually that 'something' is some information you don't want the interviewer to know. And that's exactly their reason for using this common tactic.

Think about it as a game of tennis. You've returned the serve and the ball is in your opponent's court. All you have to do is wait patiently.

—— Evaluating the interviewer ——

If you do your research properly, by the time you enter the interviewer's office, you should know some basic things about him/her. The name, the position and possibly some details of her work history, achievements, personality. These details should be the base for your analysis. You have to predict what kind of person he or she is, what is he or she looking for in the applicant, etc. However, in most cases it's almost impossible to get this type of information beforehand. Therefore, that evaluation has to be done during the interview. The sooner you get the crucial information, the better, for it can help you to frame your answers and 'fine tune' your performance during the later stages of the interview.

The tactic to remember here is called 'AAA'.

1. Anticipate   2. Adapt   3. Act

Anticipate the interviewer's questions, reactions, attitudes, fears, problems.
Adapt to the interviewer's style, manners, views, attitude. Try to share his or her values and get into his or her line of thinking.
Act upon the feedback from the interviewer. Use the clues he or she will be giving you to your advantage. If he or she is inclined towards, say

capital accounting, place the emphasis on that aspect of your accounting experience.

Another major objective of evaluating and monitoring the interviewer is constantly to keep track of how well you are doing so that you can recognise negative developments as early as possible. That way you can reverse them in your favour and pick up the indicators of positive feedback in order to reinforce further the good impressions.

Interviewer's body language and behaviour

As the interviewer evaluates your looks and body language, you have to play the same game in order to get some feedback on how you're doing. So, let's take a look at the basic grammar rules of the interviewer's body language and their meanings. A word of caution here: Body language is based on preconceptions and stereotypes. The same behaviour in different situations could have different meanings and therefore can mislead you into false conclusions. The explanations below are only the most common interpretations:

Inclination and posture

Leaning towards the applicant: sign of interest, involvement, positive intentions. *Good sign.*

Sitting erect. *Neutrality.*

Leaning back: sign of detachment or superiority. He may be evaluating the applicant or it could be just a sign that he's relaxed. *Mixed signals.*

Rigid posture: probably caused by a negative or defensive response to something you said. *Bad sign.*

Slumping: it may signal indifference, fatigue or rejection. *Beware.*

Openness

Arms crossed at the chest: closed or defensive attitude. *Beware.*

Clenched fists: aggressiveness, closed attitude. *Bad sign.*

Smile accompanied with an occasional nod: approval of what you are saying. *Good sign.*

Interviewer's body not facing you directly: emotional detachment or some other business on his mind. *Bad sign.*

Small signs that mean big problems

The arm supporting the head: *boredom.*
Drumming the fingers on the table: *impatience* and *irritation.*
Tapping of the feet on the floor: *impatience* and *irritation.*
Glancing at the watch: *impatience*, the end of the interview is imminent.

One common tendency among applicants when they are interviewed by a relaxed, friendly interviewer is to adopt or imitate (usually unconsciously) his behaviour. I wouldn't recommended it. Relax and behave naturally, but always maintain a professional and formal attitude. What is appropriate for the interviewer may not be (and usually isn't) acceptable behaviour for the applicant.

Recognise the interviewer's problems

During your job hunt you'll meet different types of interviewers – some of them will be personnel managers, personnel officers or professional recruitment consultants. They can be called professional interviewers. However, there is another group you are likely to meet: managers, supervisors, chief engineers, team leaders or professionals in various disciplines, but not in recruitment.

For some of the people in the second group, interviewing may not be the easiest of tasks. Some of them will feel uneasy because they don't have much experience in interviewing. They may run out of questions to ask or may have to consult the company's procedures and policies book constantly in order to follow the prescribed format and ask every candidate the same set of questions.

Some interviewers rely on your résumé as the backbone of the conversation and some talk too much because they don't know what questions to ask and how to interpret them, so they rely mostly on their 'gut feeling'.

Despite differences in background and in personal interviewing style and techniques, there is one common fear among interviewers: the mistake of hiring the wrong person. Should they select you for the job and you, for whatever reason, do not perform, or leave for greener pastures after only a few months, they would find it very difficult to face their boss and justify their selection. It would make them look incompetent and not very

WINNING AT JOB INTERVIEWS

thorough in their selection procedures. That is why your every gesture, every answer and every question has to convey the same message: 'I'm the right person for the job, I can make you look good in your bosses' eyes and I'm here to stay.' Remember that.

Always try to make the interviewer comfortable and to establish a cordial contact. Show your friendly side. Avoid long pauses and aggressive or pushy questions, statements or gestures. Make the interviewers feel your respect for them and show your appreciation for the opportunity to talk to them.

Basic interviewer personalities and how to treat them

> *Knowing something about the interviewer is as important as knowing everything about yourself.*

In order to use the right strategy in your dealings with a particular interviewer, you have to form an opinion about that person quickly. You have only two to three minutes for an initial analysis. This is the time it takes to establish initial contact and start a question and answer 'session'. Look for the clues:

The surroundings: office, decor, furniture, books, pictures on the walls, trophies, awards, quotations on the walls, photographs on the table, writings on the whiteboard, etc . . .

The interviewer: the appearance, age, body posture, clothes, accent, facial expressions . . .

Most interviewers could be classified into basic personality types. However, interbreeds are more common. Here are the characteristics of the main groups:

The professional

The professional is an experienced interviewer. She comes out her office to greet you in a pleasant and friendly manner. Once in her office, she makes you feel relaxed and comfortable. For the first minute or two she talks about traffic jams, the weather, your problems in finding the building or any other 'small' topic, just to break the barrier.

She will ask only relevant questions, avoiding trick questions and an interrogatory style. She will maintain an attitude of respect and understanding. The questions are formulated in a precise and concise way, using simple language. She knows what she wants to find out about you and she usually accomplishes her mission without you figuring out her subtle moves and tactics. This type of interviewer is very hard to handle, but is also human and some emotions will show, giving you the valuable clues.

Tactics: This is what all interviewers should look and act like. I haven't met too many of them, but there are some around. It's more likely that you'll meet them in personnel departments of big or progressive companies.

The interrogator

This interviewer probably watched too many 'Gestapo' movies in his younger days. He tends to fire a series of quick and short questions at the candidate and expects an immediate response. By doing that he tests the applicant's behaviour in stressful situations and saves time in the process. He probably doesn't enjoy interviewing and isn't genuinely interested in job candidates.

It is very likely that you'll be facing a sunny window or a brightly lit lamp (just to test your nerves). You may even be kept waiting longer than usual outside the office, for the same purpose.

Tactics: Be optimistic and positive, and sound that way, too. Think about yourself as a professional actor who acts in front of a hostile and unreceptive audience. Be a real professional. Don't take any short-cuts; take your time and answer questions the way you practised. Don't allow the interviewer to hurry you or make you feel uncomfortable. Ask lots of questions whenever you can. Attack is the best form of defence.

The formalist

Spontaneity is not in her vocabulary. She follows the interview evaluation sheet as if it was The Bible. She reads the questions in a monotonous and mechanical fashion and very seldom deviates from her course.

That rigid atmosphere puts most candidates off, they often feel tense and tend to adopt her behavioural style and produce short and dull answers, which only adds to their disadvantage. Do not fall into that trap. Relax and perform your 'play' properly. Take your time to answer and do not rush.

Tactics: Do not pay too much attention to that inflexible behaviour. Just try to be friendly and fire your shots as you practised them. Don't be intimidated by long pauses. Once you say what you wanted to say, wait for her to say something. The ball will be in her court. Don't volunteer any unnecessary information.

The psychologist

The psychologist is probably a failed medical student who is pretending that he holds a degree in psychology. He uses quasi-psychological 'analytical' methods, usually paying more attention to your nonverbal response than to what you actually say. Questions will be slightly different to the standard ones. He may ask you about your parents, your childhood, your purpose in life, etc. Some of the less common questions in Chapter 6 will be used. You will recognise him, for he sounds pretentious and constantly tries to show off his ego.

Tactics: Stay composed and ask for further clarification if you don't understand the question or if it's to broad. He will welcome the chance to elaborate further on his nebulous questions and be grateful for that.

The smooth talker

The 'silky' is the organisation's man. He is here to lure you into the magic world of his firm. As an interviewer, he'll probably make a good impression on you, because he won't ask too many hard questions. That's his job. This type thrives in particular industries, especially where high staff turnover or shortages of labour are a constant problem.

Tactics: Treat him as a salesman. If the deal promised sounds too good to be true, it probably is. If you accept his offer, get everything in writing. But, before that, dictate your terms to test his flexibility and advance your bargaining position.

The disorganised type

The office is generally in a mess. In some cases he may even be late for the interview. Enormous quantities of paper are piled up on the desk, which makes it difficult to find your application. It is not easy for him to organise his thoughts, especially if the conversation is frequently interrupted by phone calls or his secretary.

In this case, there is an opportunity for you to take the interview under your control, naturally, without letting the interviewer realise it. If you feel frustrated and think that this disorganised interview format may prove disadvantageous to you, suggest rescheduling the meeting for another time that will be more convenient to the interviewer.

Tactics: The disorganised type is usually friendly and flexible, which gives you a chance to present yourself in a proper manner, if you can handle the messy atmosphere around you.

The pretentious type

This interviewer has his nose high in the air. He likes interviewing because he gets somebody's undivided attention for an hour or so. He often speaks more than other types of interviewers, uses complex words, and tends to ask complicated questions to test your knowledge. He usually tries to keep his distance, so don't expect too much friendliness.

The good old humble approach is probably the best strategy here. Resist adopting his style. For a very strange reason, most people are very sensitive to flaws they possess themselves!

Tactics: Don't be intimidated by his apparent knowledge and 'advanced' interviewing methods. Know your lines, but don't pretend that you know everything, otherwise you may become like him.

The parent

The parent is usually female in her late forties or fifties, but there are some male specimens around. She is often very friendly and approachable. Her parental instincts make her adopt a specific way of treating younger applicants, who will be pampered and counselled and advised on every possible matter, if they give her an opportunity to display her maternal qualities.

Tactics: Although this type of interviewer is not particularly dangerous, you have to be composed and project maturity and apparent confidentiality. Because of her personality, she tends to elicit confidential information from naïve applicants very easily. She wants you to trust her and take your mask off. Your task is to make her believe she succeeded. That's what apparent confidentiality means. Stick to your lines, just say them in such a way that will make her think you are the most honest person around.

Interviewers' weaknesses and inconsistencies

In a hierarchy every employee tends to rise to his level of incompetence.

Laurence J. Peter

This observation is certainly true for some interviewers. They have no training in interviewing and recruiting techniques, yet they are employed to recruit staff. A recipe for disaster. Being amateurs themselves, their main concern in most cases is how to avoid making mistakes in hiring. The direct cost of these mistakes are measured in tens of thousands of pounds. That is the reason most interviewers are very cautious these days. Most of them know what type of person they want and what sort of answers they want to hear. Your role, as a candidate or interviewee, is to go there, tell them what they want to hear and reassure them that:

- you can and will do a good job for them;
- you will make them look good in their bosses' eyes;
- you will justify their decision to hire you by your performance and achievements.

Factors that affect the outcome

The validity and outcome of a job interview can be affected by a wide range of factors. Most of those factors are due to the highly subjective nature of the interviewing process. The main factors are:

- First impressions do count. Interviewers tend to make up their minds about candidates very early in the process. The order in which they receive information has an impact on the decisions.
- The previous applicants affect the interviewer's impression of the subsequent candidates.
- Physical looks of applicants influence the outcome. Physically attractive candidates have better chances of getting jobs.
- Negative information receives more of the interviewer's attention than positive data. Most interviewers use the negative to screen the applicants, turning the interview into a series of 'knockout' questions.
- Various interviewers place different values on the same information. Some emphasise communication skills, some work experience, some academic results, etc.
- Insufficient knowledge of the position and inexperience in interviewing may result in overlooking some important factors and over-emphasising the unimportant ones.

The clonal effect

First-rate people hire first-rate people; second-rate people hire third-rate people.

Leo Rosten

Every time employers intend to hire someone, two basic things are considered: one is the candidate's competency and ability to do the job; the other is the fit between the individual and the organisation. The employers ask themselves: will the candidate fit into the existing structure and become a productive member of the work force? In the process of doing that, they compare candidates with:

1   themselves;

2   former employees in the same job;

3   prevalent stereotypes and preconceptions for the particular position.

The clonal effect is the tendency among managers and recruiters to hire people they understand, trust, feel comfortable with and who are the most predictable to them. In short, people like themselves. They are looking for people with whom they can get along, communicate well and share common values. They try to multiply themselves by hiring candidates with similar backgrounds, from the same part of the country, and of the same gender and age group.

You have probably noticed that most car salesmen look alike, they behave in a very similar manner, they use the same vocabulary, share the same values. Move to the next group, say, lawyers, and you see clones again: black suits, black leather briefcases, white shirts, complex choice of words, a tendency to argue about everything with everybody, etc. The list goes on and on.

The clonal effect can make it very difficult for immigrants, minorities, women, people from different backgrounds to get hired. The best they can do is try to emulate the perceived stereotypes for the job.

Stereotypes

Stereotypes are preconceived, questionable ideas, views and opinions of other people, their origin, race, age, gender, background, physical looks, habits, marital status or any other trait.

They are frequently used by suspense and romance novelists and job interviewers. Stereotypes can work for you and against you. Unfortunately, there is nothing much you can do about most of them, like your race, sex, background and body shape. You can modify and neutralise the others.

Neutralising stereotypes is easily done through proper design of your résumé. Never write your weight, height, religion, number of children, type of car and other similar irrelevant details on your résumé. Although most people include data such as age, marital status and nationality, you can omit it without hesitation.

Some typical stereotypes that may affect you in a hiring process:

- Tall and skinny people are nervous and impatient.
- Fat people are lazy. Sloppy body means sloppy mind.
- People who don't drink are a bit strange.

- Women are too emotional and therefore unpredictable.
- People with beards are introverts and misfits.
- Unemployed people would accept any job.
- People who have changed jobs frequently in the past will continue to do so.
- Single people tend to change jobs more often. They are less stable and highly mobile, therefore can not be expected to stay with the same employer for too long.
- People with accents cannot be trusted.

The halo effect

In the selection process, employers interview more than one candidate. The number can range from two to twenty, or even more. At the end of that process it is impossible for the interviewers to remember all candidates clearly. The fact (substantiated by research statistics) is that the candidates interviewed later in the process have a much better chance of getting a job.

> *The last person interviewed has a distinct advantage, because the interviewer will remember him or her more clearly.*

Targeted selection interviews try to avoid this problem by forcing the interviewees to write their answers in a predefined format, in a space provided on the interview sheet. Still, it isn't possible to eliminate this inconsistency. To forget is a natural human tendency. This is one of the reasons why the 'Thank you' note after the interview is so important. It reminds the interviewer of you. Refer to Chapter 8 for more details.

Furthermore, you can usually arrange the interview for a later date. Don't be in 'the first bunch'. If you can, try to be among the last candidates to be interviewed. That can sometimes give you a distinct edge over your competitors.

Inexperience – being conned by a professional interviewee

The first axiom of competency:

> *The potential for a competent interviewee to manage and manipulate an incompetent interviewer is far greater than for an incompetent interviewer to manage a competent interviewee.*

Professional interviewees know how to present themselves as model employees. They understand the qualities that are attractive to employers and frame their interview performances accordingly. For you, this book is the best starting point towards achieving the goal of becoming 'one of them'. For me, this book is a ticket to interviewers' black lists. But, that's life.

'The professionals' often manage to secure jobs for which they 'just' qualify. They leave other, much more qualified and competent opponents far behind, because they realise the most important fact in interviewing:

> *People who can talk well about themselves, their experience, education and achievements, and who can project (I didn't say possess) integrity, sincerity and real interest in employers, are the ones who get jobs. The other, often more educated, more hard-working, smarter or more experienced candidates who do not know how to sell themselves, don't get what they deserve – the best jobs! What an irony!*

The common perception among some inexperienced interviewers and most candidates is that job interviews should be formal 'question and answer' sessions, with interviewers controlling the situation at all times. Job interviews should be more than that – a mutual assessment and open exchange of information. A resemblance to a tennis match is apparent – the candidates should take initiative and gain some control over the interview, otherwise they would constantly be at the receiving end, trying to return the interviewer's serves. Professional interviewees use this tactic successfully. Interviews are very elusive and deceitful encounters. Both parties are selling hard. Interviewers often promote rotten, dull jobs with no future or advancement opportunities as 'first-class deals'. You have similar rights in selling yourself.

4

INTERVIEW FORMATS
— AND EVALUATION —
METHODS

——————— Screening interviews ———————

Employers use screening interviews to determine whether the candidate
has sufficient basic qualifications and experience to warrant a formal
interview. Usually they are not targeted to a specific job and are used to
streamline the walk-in candidates. Normally, this type of interview is
conducted by one interviewer and the duration is generally limited to
between fifteen and thirty minutes.

In the current economic climate, characterised by high unemployment,
screening interviews are quickly regaining their importance. In times of
high employment screening interviews are a less common form of pre-
selection. In some industries and for some vocations, screening interviews are an essential part of the selection process.

—— Campus recruiting interviews ——

Interviews conducted by campus recruiters could be classified as a special form of screening interview. Instead of the applicants coming to the company, the company sends a recruiter, usually a personnel officer, to interview them. This is not an easy job, owing to the need to interview so many applicants in a relatively short time.

The recruiter gives basic information about the organisation, its operations and goals, and specific positions that are available for young graduates, including details on the length and structure of company's graduate training programs.

———— Telephone interviews ————

Telephone interviews mostly serve as screening interviews. I had only two telephone interviews in my career. The first one was with a large government organisation in Sydney. There were three interviewers on the other line and each one of them asked me one or two questions. The whole conversation lasted for about fifteen minutes. Believe it or not, I was offered the job, but I didn't take it.

The second one took place recently. It was just like any one-on-one interview – I had to answer twenty or so questions, the interviewer was (judging by pauses after each of my answers) taking notes and the whole session lasted for more than an hour. The company involved is in the oil and gas business, so he wasn't worried about the phone bill. The outcome – I didn't get the job, probably because I couldn't use my selling techniques over the phone.

If you ever get a job over the phone, there are only two reasons:

1   The employer was in a hurry to fill the vacancy by employing (almost) anybody, in which case you should ask yourself why that was the case. Would you take on a job that nobody else wanted?

— 79 —

2 You've mastered your interviewing skills and become a real professional in selling yourself over the phone. Congratulations!

In both cases, beware. If you were an employer, investing, say £30,000 in a new employee (one year's salary and benefits), wouldn't you like to at least meet your future employee before offering him/her a job?

If possible, avoid telephone interviews. For something this important, you need face-to-face communication. If the employer is genuinely interested in you, they should invite you for a proper interview and pay your travel expenses, if necessary.

Group interviews

Group interviews are not common, but some companies use them to evaluate a whole group of candidates at the same time. There are usually two or more interviewers, as it isn't easy for one person to evaluate five or more applicants at the same time. This interview format makes it easier for the employer to compare the applicants and determine the ones who project themselves best in the competitive atmosphere.

The group interviews are designed to intimidate candidates and evaluate them under awkward and stressful conditions. Here are a few points to remember if you want to give a good impression in these interviews:

- Stay composed and maintain your poise.
- Learn from other candidates' responses – you'll have more time to evaluate the interviewer and your competitors while they answer questions – use that knowledge in formulating your answers.
- Don't criticise your opponents' answers, attitudes and opinions.
- Don't be intimidated by the whole situation.

Panel interviews

The panel interview is probably the most common evaluation method used by employers (especially the big organisations) when recruiting professional and managerial personnel. By using a panel of three or four interviewers, they try to establish an unbiased and objective picture of a candidate.

The interviewers usually come from different departments or sections of the company. One of them will lead the group and frame the whole session. Almost without exception, that person will be the personnel officer, personnel manager or somebody with a similar title, for they regard themselves best qualified to 'hire and fire'. Other members of the panel will include the immediate supervisor or manager, who hires the candidate to work in his/her section, the department manager and, in some cases (if needed), a specialist whose task is to evaluate the candidate's specialist knowledge.

This type of interview tends to be highly structured. Each member of the panel evaluates a specific area of the candidate's background, and by doing that, the employers are assured that all important points, such as the candidate's experience, qualifications and personality, will be explored and evaluated.

When asked a question by one of the interviewers, devote more attention to that person, but also maintain eye contact with the other members of the panel while answering the question. Generally, try to divide your attention equally between all of them. Don't speak to the leader only, or the person who asked a question. Try to remember their names and 'who is who' in the organisation. Frame your answers accordingly and modify your approach. If you talk to an accountant, try to think like him, when you talk to an engineer, talk in his (technical) terms.

One-on-one interviews

In this case only one person evaluates the candidates and makes a decision who to hire for the job, either alone or after consultation with upper management. Although there are always some exceptions, this interview format is mostly used by smaller companies and when hiring non-professional personnel (secretaries, tradesmen, so called 'blue collar workers', etc.).

In most of these cases the qualifications and skills of the candidates are more clearly defined and, therefore, easier to measure than those of professional employees (engineers, lawyers, scientists, accountants).

The interviewer is most likely to be the immediate supervisor or a manager to whom the position reports. The interview will be the best opportunity for both parties to evaluate each other.

Lunch interviews

If you have an interview away from your home town, you will probably be taken out for lunch, sometimes before, but usually after the actual interview. In most cases a quick tour around the company's premises will be organised and the 'official' interview will take place. After lunch, there will possibly be some time left for another tour through the company, in order to meet other managers and employees, and maybe a short sight-seeing trip around town, for candidates to get a feeling about the place. The scenarios will vary from case to case, but there are some general rules to observe:

1   Always bear in mind that the interviewer will keep evaluating you, no matter where you go or what you do.

2   At lunch, follow basic common-sense:
   - Eat where the interviewer wishes. Let him choose the place.
   - Don't drink alcohol, even if the interviewer orders wine or beer. You'll need clear mind to present yourself in the right way.
   - Choose a meal that is easy to eat, is not messy, does not leave you with foul breath and is priced in the same range as the interviewer's meal.
   - Let the interviewer pay for the meal. It's part of re-cruiting expenses and nobody will expect you to honour the bill.

3   Maintain your poise and don't become too friendly with the interviewers.

——————— Situational interviews ———————

Some employers go beyond conventional interviewing techniques and try to evaluate the applicants' skills through situational evaluation. Behavioural simulations and job replica tests are sometimes used for that purpose.

Behavioural simulations are used to test the applicants in certain areas which are difficult to evaluate through normal question and answer sessions. They can take various forms, such as sales presentations for the evaluation of sales people, interview simulations for people who will be dealing with customers or clients, scheduling exercises for people in project control, purchasing, logistics, etc.

The job replica tests are a special type of behavioural simulation. They are designed to help evaluate the candidate's skills in performing tasks directly related to the position. A typing or shorthand test for a secretary, driving test for a driver, or a language test for a translator, are examples of job replica tests.

—— Targeted selection interviews ——

The objective of a targeted selection interview is to provide specific information about the candidate, on predefined dimensions, which have been identified as important for a particular position. The employer identifies the critical skills, qualifications and personal traits needed to perform in the job. The interview questions are designed in advance to target those areas and to allow for in-depth analysis of the candidate. The whole process is based on the assumption that past behaviour is the best indication of future behaviour.

A whole chapter in this book is devoted to these targeted areas and the most common questions are analysed in depth. Some possible answers are suggested. Employers are not interested in theoretical or hypothetical answers. They want to hear about your experience. Each example from your past has to address the following elements:

- The situation that existed (problem you had to solve or task you had to perform).
- The action you took in order to solve the problem or perform the task.
- The result of your actions (the outcome of your efforts).

This evaluation method is becoming very popular with many companies, especially with those in the resources sector (mining, mineral processing, oil and gas). After a couple of interviews, it became obvious to me that they used the same consultant to devise a list of questions, for the lists are almost identical, and emphasis is placed on the same values. This makes it much easier for astute job hunters to prepare themselves for the interview.

To you, the applicant, the major advantage of this interviewing technique is consistency. All applicants are asked the same questions, so they'll be judged by the same criteria. The main disadvantage is the lack of flexibility. Individual differences tend to be ignored or overlooked if the interviewers don't ask pertinent questions, probing for more revealing answers.

Applicants usually feel the rigid structure of this interview type, which tends to make them less relaxed, and the whole process is dominated by the interviewers.

A highly structured interview, such as targeted selection, is the most time-efficient of all types. For an inexperienced interviewer, it is also the easiest to conduct. That must be the reason for its survival in the battle against more efficient, flexible and intimate methods.

Unstructured interviews

The unstructured or unguided interview is a less rigid encounter during which the applicant sets the pace and, to a certain extent, dictates the progress of the interview. Questions asked tend to follow the leads given by the applicant. This gives you the leading edge, puts the control in your hands and makes it easier to expand on your strong points and avoid any problem areas. This interview type tends to be used by two groups of recruiters – the inexperienced greenhorns and the very experienced head-hunters.

The first group uses it for the simple reason that they can't control the interview so they leave it to the candidate to set the pace and sell themselves. Experienced interviewers, on the other hand, use this technique to evaluate, above other attributes, the candidate's character and personal traits. They can read between the lines and make conclusions not only about what the applicant said, but also about things that the applicant did not say, either because they did not know how to say it, or because they were trying to conceal something.

Evaluation methods: the mystery revealed

It is far from easy to evaluate a person in an hour or so. Résumés, various interview formats, evaluation methods, psychological tests, reference checks and a whole range of other tools have been used by employers in the selection process. In order to compare applicants, identify their strong and weak points and match them against the predefined criteria for a particular job, various evaluation methods have been developed by recruiting personnel.

Basic concerns

There are three basic concerns for employers when recruiting:

1   Can a candidate do a job?

2   Will the candidate do the job?

3   Will the candidate fit into a workplace team?

Your task is to convince and reassure the employer that the answer to each of these questions is **yes**!

Areas for evaluation

There is no universal evaluation method that could be applied to every applicant and every position. Different employers place different values on the same skills and abilities. However, there are dimensions that are common to almost every evaluation method. Let us take a look at some of them and identify the employer's line of thinking when assessing your background:

Qualifications: Does the applicant have the formal qualifications to do the job? Does she know how to do the job? Are her qualifications recognised in the industry as appropriate for this particular position?

Work experience: Does the applicant have relevant work experience? How much experience does she have and how could we benefit from that experience?

Motivation: How motivated is the candidate? What motivates her – money, sense of achievement, praise, title, working conditions? Is she a self-starter or does she need constant supervision?

Communication skills: Can the candidate express herself in writing and in good grammatical form? Can she express herself in individual and group situations orally? Is she a good listener? Can she effectively communicate her ideas and explain and present tasks?

Maturity and emotional stability: Is she able to cope with stress and pressures at work and in private? Is she a mature and responsible person who can make decisions and assume responsibility? Is she emotionally stable and fair and consistent in her dealings with superiors and subordinates?

Sound health: How good is the candidate's health? Is she likely to be productive for a long time? Is she going to be on sick-leave frequently?

The information employers need

The aim of job interviews, especially targeted selection interviews, is to collect job-related behaviour examples from the applicants' history. The

interviewers require three types of information for each example in order
to evaluate the candidate:

1   the **situation** that existed or **task** that had to be performed;

2   the specific **action** taken or not taken (and why or why not);

3   the **results** or consequences of the **action** (or the lack of it).

The interviewers using this method have to make sure that only complete examples are collected. You, the candidate, have to frame your
answers accordingly and address all three issues.

Incomplete answers

By using this method employers try to eliminate 'false' answers, which
don't reflect the candidate's past experience. These false answers could
be classified as follows:

- vague answers;
- theoretical answers;
- future-orientated answers;
- incomplete answers.

Vague answers lack clarity, simplicity, coherence or focus on the issue.
Applicants quite often omit some relevant details, either intentionally (if
the information is unfavourable), or by forgetting to mention them
(unintentionally).

Most applicants are good at giving theoretical answers. It isn't difficult to
tell the interviewer what you would do in a certain situation, what you
could do to solve a problem, or how you would handle an obstacle. In
most cases the answer is obvious to an experienced interviewee. This is
where attentive listening to the way interviewers phrase questions and
looking for clues in their behaviour is invaluable.

Future-orientated answers tell the employer what you are planning to do
in the future. This information is not necessarily useless, but since most
employers tend to predict future behaviour on the basis of your past
performance, the future-orientated answers are perceived as much less
important than required 'factual' answers.

Incomplete answers lack one or more of the three main components (situation or task that the applicant performed, action taken by applicant or results of that action).

— Psychological and aptitude tests —

What is the point of giving the applicants a psychological test that bears no relation to the job for which they have been considered? How do we define 'personality'? Which personalities are suited to which jobs? What happens with multiple-choice questions when there is no suggested option that matches the true feeling of the candidate?

These and many other questions started debates about the relevance of psychological and aptitude tests in the recruiting process and led to their ban in the United States. Basically, they did not meet the requirements of the equal opportunity laws. The tests tried to assess the applicants' personalities and their suitability for particular jobs by asking vague questions which were open to interpretation and enabled employers to justify their opinions, biases and final choices.

We don't have enough space here to explain all tests and methods in detail, so let's just take a quick look at the main types of tests, as expertly presented in the book *Effective Recruitment & Selection Practices*, by R L Crompton and A R Nankervis:

- General ability tests, which measure verbal, numerical, speed, spatial, strength, coordination or perceptual skills.
- Specific aptitude tests or work samples, such as keyboard, technical, foreign language, etc, skills.
- Personality (or temperament) tests, which are designed to assess overall 'personality' characteristics such as 'introversion versus extroversion', 'initiative' or 'creativity'.

It is essential to mention here the two basic types of testing, *psychometric* and *psychodynamic*. Psychometric tests compare the individual with a standard population profile defined by test standards. In psychodynamic testing, the emphasis is placed on the way a person reacts, therefore it represents a more qualitative approach.

Some of the most popular tests used are The Defence Mechanism Test (DMT) which originated in Sweden, The Ravens Test, The Watson-Glaser Test, and The Colour Test.

In the DMT test, a candidate is given a large sheet of paper with twenty empty squares. In a split second a slide appears in a box. The candidate, looking into the box, has to draw his impression of the picture on slide.

The Ravens Test uses a set of matrices of increasing complexity in order to test the candidate's visual problem-solving ability.

The Watson-Glaser Test, in a similar way, tests the candidate's ability to think logically, solve problems, evaluate information and make decisions.

In the Colour Test, candidates have to arrange differently coloured tiles in accordance to a few rules. The final product are two pyramids, whose pattern reveals details about the candidates' characters and intellectual inclinations.

5

DOS AND DON'TS IN INTERVIEWING

Before the interview

- Study this book.
- Research the company you are or will be interviewing with.
- Find out as much as possible about the job you've applied for.
- Prepare your own customised answers based on model answers in the next chapter, and on the particulars of the job.
- Practise your answers, either alone or with a partner playing the role of the interviewer. If needed, record your sessions on a video or audio tape and try to improve your accent, diction, tone of voice and fluency.
- Prepare your interview clothes and try various combinations. Select the outfit that complies with normal business standards and allows you to feel comfortable and confident while wearing it.
- A day or two before the interview, visit the premises where you'll be interviewed, to assess the travelling time and to familiarise yourself with the surroundings. You'll feel more comfortable when you arrive for the interview.
- Arrange to have the interview at the best time for you. If you feel your best in the morning, don't arrange the interview for the

afternoon. Avoid Mondays and Fridays if you can – the interviewers may feel rushed, tired or irritated.

- Check the condition of your car or the public transport timetable, to allow extra time for unpredictable events. Being late for an interview is a mortal sin.
- Have a haircut, trim your beard (man), manicure your nails, whiten your teeth. Do anything necessary to improve your looks.
- Have a light snack. Never walk into an interview on an empty stomach. Don't eat too much, either. The last thing you need is feeling sleepy or sluggish before and during the interview.
- If you're a nervous person or just 'stage shy' have a cup of strong, black coffee. Caffeine is a stimulant and can give you an extra edge. I personally used capsules with herbal extracts for their tranquillising effect. Both methods are good, but you have to be careful not to take too much. Experiment beforehand.
- While waiting for the interview to start, practise relaxation techniques. Breathe deeply and try to relax.
- If your palms sweat, make sure they are dry when you shake hands with the interviewer. Sweaty palms are the first bad impression people usually make.

——— During the interview ———

- Be businesslike and professional.
- Don't talk too much.
- Listen carefully and watch for any clues. Feedback from the interviewer is a valuable tool in framing your answers.
- Use strong, positive reasons when explaining gaps and changes in your career.
- Basically, be truthful, but be prepared to 'bend' the truth if it suits the circumstances. However, project honesty and sincerity.
- Ask relevant questions that will help you appear intelligent, educated and experienced. Your questions should make the interviewer aware that you have done some research on his company, which will help you to be seen as an ambitious and resourceful person.
- Never take books to an interview, (unless specifically asked to do so) especially not this one or any other on interviewing or job hunting.

- Establish and maintain eye contact with the interviewer.
- Smile. Be friendly and relaxed. Project optimism.
- Don't try to sell yourself too strongly.
- Never criticise your previous or present employer.
- Never indicate that you are desperate to get a job.
- Never make jokes.
- Never bring your friend, partner, children or anybody else with you to the interview, not even to the waiting room.
- Never talk about your personal life, business secrets or the internal affairs of other companies, such as your present or former employers. Being trustworthy is a rare commodity and the interviewer will appreciate the fact that you may refuse (by politely avoiding the question) to answer some questions.
- Sit straight in your chair or lean slightly forward. That way you project interest and attention.
- Never play with your keys, hair, tie, watch, pen or any other item.
- Don't fidget with your hands, drum your fingers, keep your hands in pockets, scratch your head or crack your knuckles.
- Never eat, drink, smoke, chew gum or pick your teeth.
- Never wear dark glasses, a hat or dental braces.
- Never smell of alcohol, garlic or any strong odour.
- Don't make comments about the interviewer's office, furnishings, the receptionist, air-conditioning, etc.
- Never answer a question if you don't understand it fully. Ask for further clarification.
- Never use phrases such as 'I don't know', 'I don't think so', 'I disagree', 'What kind of question is that?', 'Why do you want to know that?' or any similar statement or question.
- Bring the conversation to a human level. Don't just plainly supply the data the interviewer wants to hear. Use examples, feelings, analogies, comparisons . . . Use fresh words, not the usual common phrases and clichés.
- Be persuasive. Speak in terms of the benefits the employer would gain if you were hired. Talk in terms of their requirements.
- If you don't know an answer to a particular question, openly admit so. Don't be tempted to answer it. Nobody knows everything.
- Never use the interviewer's first name. Adjust the formality of your behaviour to suit the interviewer's.

- If you feel that the interviewer is insulting you or if you feel manipulated, leave immediately. Your dignity should be more important than any job. If they treat you that way before offering you a job, can you imagine what your life would be like once you started working for them?
- Never bring up the question of salary and benefits yourself. Wait for the interviewer to start discussing money matters, otherwise you may be viewed as interested only in money. When negotiating your salary, make sure that you don't mention the amount first. Whoever comes up with the first figure is disadvantaged in the negotiation process.
- Although some specialists on interviewing disagree, I think it is a good practice to take notes during the interview (of course, only while the interviewer is speaking). This should help you in case you have to come back for a second interview or to evaluate the job later, should you have more than one job offer. Just make sure you don't overdo it. Your notes should be as brief as possible to enable you to maintain eye contact with the interviewer at all times.

After the interview

- Always write a polite 'Thank you' note to the interviewer. Consider this format:

Arthur Renton
25 Bridge Street
Cambridge CB1 1CB

Mrs Ann Kennedy
Roberts and Partners
97 Eastleigh Road
Chelmsford
Essex
CM4 4MC

26 August 1994

Dear Mrs Kennedy,

Thank you for the opportunity to talk to you about the position of Litigation Lawyer with your firm. After discussing this career opportunity with you I feel that Roberts and Partners is the right environment in which I could utilise my skills and knowledge and contribute to your Company's success.

I would be proud to be associated with such a reputable firm and would consider it a privilege to be on your team.

Yours sincerely,

Arthur Renton
Arthur Renton

- Record all details about the interview in your 'job file' as soon as possible, preferably immediately after the interview. This can prove extremely valuable in the future, for it will enable you to evaluate your performance and avoid costly mistakes. The following information should prove useful:
  - the name of the company and the interviewer;
  - general impression of the company, the job and the interviewer;
  - specific interviewer's questions and areas of interest;

— interviewer's feedback and reactions to your answers;
— interviewer's comments about your résumé, your education or employment history;
— specific job-related information supplied by the interviewer;
— interviewer's body language and non-verbal communication.

- Immediately after the interview, analyse your performance and write down your specific comments and self-impressions. These will be extremely valuable in preparing for job interviews in the future. You may even have another interview with the same company.

To summarise, these are some of the points you should cover in your post-interview self-appraisal:

— your best answers (judging by your interpretation of the interviewer's response);
— your poorest answers;
— your body language and behaviour;
— your questions, their relevance and appropriateness;
— other relevant details (did you arrive on time, the way you greeted the interviewer);
— the things you would change or introduce if you could do it again.

- Be persistent. If you were unsuccessful interviewing with a particular employer, don't automatically assume that the company has no openings for you.

I had three interviews with my present employer in two years. While I was unsuccessful on the first two occasions, for various reasons, the third interview resulted in a job offer. The experience gained in the first two interviews (although with different interviewers every time) enabled me to think in terms of benefits to the employer, to prepare my answers and polish my performance for the third and final encounter. As you may have guessed, I was selected for the job among more than forty applicants, some probably as experienced and qualified for the job as I was. By the time I had the last interview, I had prepared a folder containing the crucial information – the questions I was asked, the answers I gave, the names of interviewers, as well as many important details about the company, its operations and philosophy. Before the third appraisal, I studied the information available and prepared myself properly. The preparations obviously paid off.

6

QUESTIONS, ANSWERS AND EYE-OPENERS

Hard questions must have hard answers.

Plutarch

This chapter deals with some typical interview questions. There is a limited number of questions you could be asked to answer. They may vary slightly in content and the order of questions could differ, but the best answers will always be the best answers.

Behind each question you have to recognise the interviewer's fear or concern, which is basically why they are asking you the question. Once the fear or concern is established, the optimal answers can be framed accordingly. My comments, printed in italics, may help you to do that.

In most questions I suggest a skeleton you may consider using in your answers. You can expand on it or change it to suit your background. Don't change it drastically, use it as a starting point for your script. For some questions, short advice is given, owing to the fact that those questions require specific answers which will reflect your occupation or your specific experience.

The interviewer's task is to evaluate various areas of your background, such as your work experience, education, communication skills, salary history, management skills, etc. The questions in this chapter are grouped together according to those areas. The order of questions asked will vary from interview to interview.

There are at least half a dozen questions in each area. There will be no need for an interviewer to ask you all of them, so you can use certain answers for other, related questions. Sometimes the question you'll be asked will comprise two questions in one, or even three or more (less likely, but possible). In this case make sure you remember all questions you were asked and answer them one by one. Most people just answer the first one and forget about the rest. Some interviewers use this tactic (asking a few questions together) to test a candidate's memory and concentration.

Some questions are more important than others, because of the impact they may have on the interviewer. I have called them 'knockout' questions because of their potential to get you out of interviews very quickly if not answered properly. Pay special attention to these questions.

Most interviewers use them for initial evaluation; should you 'pass' this hard part, you'll be a serious candidate for the job. Should you 'fail', you could see an abrupt end to the interview approaching.

> *As with any performance, such as acting or public speaking (job interview has elements of both), practice is of paramount importance. It's not enough to know the answers. You must be able to deliver them in the best possible way.*

The system is simple – record the questions and your own answers on tape. Play it in your spare time. Once you've remembered all questions and all answers, make another tape. This time record only the questions, leaving time for yourself to answer them. Do that in front of a mirror, observing your body language and 'delivery'.

> *Perfect practice makes perfect performance.*

Personal details

1. **Do you have a valid driver's licence?**
   If you have a valid licence:
   A: Yes, I have a full licence which is valid until 2012.
   If you don't already have a driver's licence, say you'll get one, especially if the job requires it.

2. **Have you ever been convicted for a driving offence?**
   If you have, explain the circumstances and determination not to allow it to happen again.
   A: I always drive carefully and never drink alcohol beforehand. Once I was in a hurry to be on time for an appointment and lost one penalty point for driving just above the speed limit. Otherwise my driving record is clean.

3. **Do you have any chronic health conditions or disabilities?**
   This question is illegal. If you choose to answer, consider something along these lines:
   A: My health is generally very good. I exercise regularly and control my weight. I have had (*slightly high blood pressure, diabetes, asthma*) for a few years but I control it, so I haven't had any of the usual symptoms and it has never affected my performance at work.
   or
   My health is excellent. I have no chronic health conditions (*much better answer*).

4. **Do you own a car? If so, what make and model?**
   A: At the moment I don't have a car, because I have sold my old one, but if the job requires the use of a reliable and presentable car, I am prepared to buy one as soon as possible.
   or
   I own the latest model of (*Escort, Cavalier, Astra*) outright.

5. **Have you done any military service?**
   Emphasise your achievements during military service, especially those which, in some way, relate to the job you are being interviewed for.

6. How far do you live from this office?

A: I live only eleven kilometres from your office. It took me just over 18 minutes to get here, which is very good if you take into account that it was the rush-hour.

7. This job would require you to move to another part of the country. Would that be a problem?

Point out that knew about the job requirements and that you are prepared to move anywhere (if you are).

A: I was aware of that fact before I applied for this position, so I discussed the issue with my partner. She/he would like to move to Gloucester as much as I would. The atmosphere of the city is very similar to our present lifestyle and we have some very good friends there, so it shouldn't take us long to settle down.

8. I can see from your résumé that you speak German and Italian. How proficient are you in these languages?

A: I studied German in primary school and in high school and found the language interesting, so I studied it further through language courses and tapes. I even spent a summer working in Germany and improving my proficiency, so now I'm fluent in German.

or

My partner is a foreign language teacher so I have learned basic Italian from her/him. I'm not very fluent, but I can read and write the language quite well.

9. Are you a member of a trade union?

If a job requires membership of a particular union, say you will apply for it immediately (if you are not a member already). If the employer's general attitude is to oppose the unions, emphasise the fact that you are purely a financial member, with no involvement in union activities.

A: I have been a member of the union for the past six years but I'm not active in the union movement or activities.

Education and training

Colleges can't produce competence, but they can produce graduates.

Anon.

1. **What college/university did you attend?**
A: I attended Boston High School in Lincoln. After my 'A' levels, I moved with my parents to Liverpool where I enrolled at the university. I graduated with honours from The Faculty of Civil Engineering.

2. **Why did you choose that particular institution?**
Most employers value practical skills much more than the theoretical ones. Emphasise that aspect in your answer.
A: I selected that university because of its competitive atmosphere and the outstanding reputation of the —— (*Engineering Department, Arts School*). The courses were well balanced, with just the right mixture of theoretical and practical topics. They encouraged students to participate in different activities and emphasised practical skills that can be applied to problems in industry.

3. **Did your family have any influence on your choice of career?**
Stress the fact that you chose your future. Having parents making decisions for you is a serious knockout factor.
A: My parents made some suggestions, but they never tried to influence my decisions. They realised that I had made up my mind and that I knew what I wanted, so they left me to decide.

4. **What was your major?**
A: I majored in _____ (*interior design, maintenance management, English literature*). I have always liked the challenges and satisfaction of that demanding but interesting profession.

5. **Do you think you made the right career choice?**
For people staying in the same occupation:

A: I am very pleased with my decision. Although I have other talents I am sure this profession suits my abilities well and enables me to utilise my knowledge and skills fully. It gives me a great sense of achievement and the rewards are adequate.

For people who are changing careers or are contemplating a change:
When I started my career as ____ (*a lawyer, interior designer*) I kept learning and growing in the job. After mastering the skills and achieving my goals in that area, I decided to gain additional experience in ____ (*mention the occupation you want to move into*). That way my creativity and flexibility was enhanced and I have achieved a range of new skills that I can use in my new career.

6. **Do you feel your education prepared you well for the challenges in the work force?**

A: My education and training gave me a solid foundation on which I built my knowledge base and gave me the confidence to face the future challenges. To achieve good results at university I had to work hard, set my goals and do my best to achieve them. The same principles apply in the work force. The problem-solving and goal-setting skills that I acquired have helped me a lot throughout my career.

7. **How did you do in school/at university?**

A: My results were above average, always in the top fifteen per cent of my class. I worked part time as well and was involved in many extracurricular activities in student clubs and societies.

8. **How did you finance your university education?**

If you worked part time to pay the fees, tell them so. It shows your determination and willingness to work hard. Scholarships and grants are not bad either. Your talents were recognised early, otherwise you wouldn't have got it.

A: Throughout my college days I worked part time to pay expenses. My parents helped a great deal and I also received a scholarship from ____.

9. **What were your favourite subjects/courses?**

Mention something related to the position you are being interviewed for.

A: I always felt great interest towards _____ (*commerce, marketing*), but when I began the course I discovered all challenges and possibilities in that area. Other related courses reinforced my interest for the subject even further and I found I had the potential to be successful in that field.

10. Did you ever need tutoring? In what subjects?
Even if you did use a tutor, don't mention it. That information cannot be checked and is not relevant to your current abilities and skills.

A: Always being one of the top students in my class I didn't need tutoring or any other help. I attended lectures and tutorials regularly and never had any particular difficulties.

11. How much knowledge gained in school/at university do you feel you could use in this job?
Ideally, all of it. Practically, only some of it. Your answer should be closer to 'all of it'.

A: This position requires knowledge and some of the skills I acquired as a student. Most of the courses I had could be directly related to this job. My knowledge of _____ and especially my background in _____ would enable me to carry out all tasks required in this job very successfully.

12. What courses in school/at university gave you the most difficulty?
Mention some subject or area that is totally irrelevant to the job you are applying for.

A: I never had a great deal of interest in _____ (*history, foreign languages, classic literature*), but I forced myself to study hard so I managed to achieve above average results.

13. What courses were the easiest ones for you?
Use the courses that are business-orientated or directly related to the job.

A: I've always liked _____ (*mathematics, physics, typing, computer programming*). I felt a great deal of pleasure preparing for those exams and my results were outstanding. Those courses were a solid foundation for my later studies and equipped me with practical skills that I used in my previous jobs.

14. Are you planning to continue your studies towards _____ (a diploma/degree/higher degree/MBA/PhD)?

A: After beginning my career I realised that in addition to my degree in _____ (*engineering, geology, law*), I needed some general business and management skills, so in _____ (*1991, 1992*) I enrolled in the MBA program at Liverpool University. I expect to graduate in two years' time. I'm putting my new skills to use applying them to my job in order to handle demanding tasks more efficiently.

15. Have you received any formal training since graduation?
By asking this question the interviewer wants to see if you have continued to expand and update your knowledge and skills. Good opportunity to score points.

A: After graduation I used every opportunity to expand my knowledge and acquire further skills. I attended various courses, workshops and seminars. Most of them were accredited courses, recognised by _____ (*The Institution of Engineers, The Association of Chartered Accountants, etc.*). Some of them were sponsored by my employers and for others I used my own money. The investment in training has really paid off, because it has enabled me to become more efficient and master new skills that I can apply directly in the job.
or

A: So far I have used every opportunity to improve my knowledge and skills through on-the-job learning and subscribing to trade magazines. This year I'm planning to enrol on a _____ course to enhance my knowledge on the subject.

Personal traits

If any young man comes to me and asks how to make his fortune, I tell him to do the same. Don't follow everybody else. Get off the beaten track. Be a little mad.

Jeno Paulucci, *How It Was to Make $100 Million in a Hurry*

Attention to detail

1. **Do you occasionally get bored while doing detailed work?**
    If you're applying for a manual job or a job that involves detailed work (design, finance, craftsmanship) this is a very appropriate question. Even if you apply for a supervisory job or a position in management (more orientated towards problem solving and decision making), you will occasionally have to deal with details.

A: I treat all my activities as an extension of the job. My daily routine requires efficiency to increase the results achieved. This efficiency includes devoting attention to details. If people can't get the little things right, how can they expect to do the big things? So, no matter how busy I am working on concepts and bigger issues, I always make checking details high priority.

2. **Do you like analytical tasks?**
A: I consider myself very good at facts and figures. I developed my mathematical and analytical skills early in the process and have been using them for quite some time. My decision to become _____ (*an accountant, a statistician, an engineer*) reflected that orientation towards facts and figures. I like the organised way of thinking and the systematic approach to problems needed when dealing with facts and figures. These skills help me in all spheres of my job.

3. **What methods do you use for controlling errors in your paperwork?**
A: Since the introduction of personal computers and software packages, such as spreadsheets and word processors, it has become much easier to control errors and mistakes. As I progress through the project, I make sure I check all the facts and figures regularly and update the necessary paperwork. If some typing is done by the secretary, I proof-read it before signing to make sure there are no errors.

4. **Tell me about times when you or your superiors found an error in your work? What was the outcome of the whole situation?**
A: I haven't made many errors in my work, owing to my attention to

detail and the attention I pay to all aspects of each task. Occasionally, when jobs had to be finished in a very short time or when not enough information was available, a minor error would creep in. On one occasion I prepared figures for the next day presentation. Just before the meeting a calculation error was discovered, so I had to correct it urgently. Fortunately, it occurred later in the process, so only a minor part of the material had to be changed and everything ended well.

5.   Do you get bored or lose interest when doing the same tasks over and over again?

A: Daily routine is more or less part of everybody's job. If my job involves repetitive work it is my responsibility to carry it out to the best of my abilities. There are some tasks that have to be done regularly and I don't regard them as boring or unchallenging. I consider all work as important and due to my workload I'm never bored or idle.

Energy

1.   When do you tend to do your best work, in the morning or in the afternoon?

Most of us have our favourite period when we feel at our best and tend to produce our best results. This question, however, tries to assess your energy level. Make sure you don't say things like: 'I do most work in the morning, because I feel exhausted after lunch and need some rest.'

A: The time of the day usually has no impact on my efficiency and energy level, but I prefer morning hours for major tasks, and late afternoon or early evening for planning, design and catching up on paperwork. I rarely get tired, even when I work overtime – it's just that some periods during the day are better suited for particular activities.

2.   How do you catch up on the work backlog after a holiday or absence from site?

Apart from testing your energy level, this question probes into your organisational skills. Frame your answer in a way which highlights your systematic approach to prioritising issues and tasks.

A: In a situation like this, I would try to spend a few hours in the office the day before I officially start work, be it Sunday or during the working week. That way I could go through the mail and messages, sort them in order of importance and urgency and plan my activities for the week ahead.

The first few days after my return are always very busy. There are people to talk to, many messages to be answered and issues to be resolved. That usually requires a lot of overtime work, but that has always been a part of my work day, especially after a long absence.

3. ✔ **What do you do with your spare time? What do you do for exercise?**

A: I always try to spend free time with my family. We either play sports, go for a walk, do some gardening or work around the house. In the evenings I pursue my hobbies or catch up on my reading. I exercise in the morning, take long walks combined with jogging, and also do some weight-lifting.

4. **What kind of tasks do you find most tiring?**
Because of the way this question is formed, it's a bit tricky to answer it favourably. Your message has to be based on the fact that you don't tire easily, no matter what kind of task you are dealing with.

5. **Have you worked on night shifts before?**
A: I have worked night shifts often in the past. If this job requires night shift work that would suit me fine.
or
A: So far I haven't worked on a night shift. However, I have often worked long hours and afternoon shifts, so if this job requires some night shift work I could do it without any problems.

6. **What are the longest hours you have ever worked?**
The answer will depend on your occupation and your particular circumstances. Don't just say: twelve hours. Explain the problem, the urgency of the situation, the skills you used at the time, etc. Expand and explain.
A: On quite a few occasions, when an urgent or important problem had to be solved or a critical task done, such as _____ (*major plant*

shutdown, urgent surgery, major equipment failure) I worked very long hours, typically _____ (*twelve, sixteen, twenty*) hours. In my profession it is necessary to put in long hours quite often so the jobs can be completed on time.

Initiative and creativity

> *There is nothing more difficult to carry out, nor more doubtful of success, nor more dangerous to handle, than to initiate a new order of things.*

Niccolo Machiavelli

- *Taking active steps to achieve goals.*
- *Active attempts to initiate action, rather than passively observing.*
- *Doing things differently and more efficiently.*
- *Attempts to achieve more than originally called for.*

Key words: ambition, drive, motivation, self-starter, innovation, peak performance.

1. **Have you ever worked alone or without direct supervision?**
   The ability to work alone is perceived as very important by interviewers. Nobody wants to employ a candidate who needs a supervisor behind his back to keep telling him what to do, when, how and why.
A: In my former job as construction foreman, I worked long hours in remote areas without direct supervision. Occasionally, I would consult a site engineer regarding a technical problem, but generally, I handled all problems and managed the work group by myself.

2. **What have you done in your current job to make it more productive or challenging?**
   This is the right time to mention ideas that you've implemented and new projects or innovations you have made at your place of work. Be specific and address the three basic elements: situation (problem), your action and the outcome.

3. **Do you think you are an innovative person? Why do you think so?**

A: I certainly try to be innovative. Whenever I have a task to accomplish or a problem to solve, I think about different ways that can lead towards the successful completion of that task, or solution to the problem. Most people choose the path of least resistance, but in the majority of cases the easiest solutions are not the best. I enjoy investigating new possibilities, considering new ways of doing things and using new methods to achieve objectives.

4. **Give me some examples of projects or tasks when you did more than normally required in your job.**
   By asking this question the interviewer will try to establish how you define a good job and evaluate your work standards.

A: To achieve peak performance, I always put in more effort than merely doing the job by the book. This comes naturally to me, as part of my work ethics. I am not happy with mediocre efforts, because they lead to mediocre results.
   Now, add an example or two from your own experience to support this opening.

5. **Tell me about some projects you generated or initiated yourself.**
   The ability to recognise problems and issues that need attention and to take action in solving or rectifying them is regarded as important by many employers. You have to convince them in your answer that you are not just a passive observer and follower, but rather a resourceful person and a self-starter.

6. **Have you found any ways of making your staff's job easier or more interesting?**
   This question is intended for supervisors or managers who control and manage a group of people. There are many new management ideas and methods, with the purpose of making jobs more interesting and challenging. You can mention successful implementation of some of these schemes or programs, such as an employee participation scheme which involved the whole group in the decision-making process, competition challenge between shifts or teams, or schemes such as 'The Employee of the Month Award'. Anything original and innovative will be a big plus for you.

7. **Are there some methods that you use that are different or some things that you do differently from other (accountants, managers, salespersons)?**
    Being original and innovative is always nice, just make sure you don't overdo it. You may be seen as unpredictable, a misfit or a weirdo. Concentrate on relatively common, not very 'exotic' methods or work practices.

A: Each creative person has his or her own techniques and means for achieving results and getting the job done, as well as little secrets that sometimes mean big success. None of them is universal and suitable for everybody. What works for you may not work for me, and vice versa.

    Now, tell them about one or two of your 'specialities', things or methods that you use because they work well for you.

Integrity

> *You've got to stand for something, or you're going to fall for anything.*
>
> John Cougar Mellencamp

- *Maintaining and observing social, ethical and organisational norms in job-related activities.*
- *The quality of being honest and upright in character.*

1. **To get the job done people sometimes have to bend the truth. Give me an example when you had to do the same thing?**
    A typical knockout question. By asking the question this way, the interviewer indicates that such behaviour is common and not necessarily negative. He even condones it. Don't fall into this trap. By doing this he wants you to admit an instance of low integrity behaviour. Fair play and personal integrity are still highly valued by interviewers, especially those of British origin. American credo is to win, British motto is to participate.

2. **Have you ever broken a company rule?**
    Another knockout question. Some employers are very sensitive where

their rules, policies and procedures are concerned. They become so indoctrinated that any individualistic approach or alternative way of doing things is viewed as major disloyalty and disobedience. Your answer here has to be: never!

A: I consider company rules, policies and procedures necessary for the efficient running of the business. They ensure that fairness, consistency and safety measures are applied across the board and that the right work environment is created and maintained. My personal policy is always to observe the rules and make sure my subordinates observe them as well.

3.   **Some sales people frequently tend to 'oversell' the product to make a sale. What is your opinion of that technique?**

A: I have never used the 'overselling' technique. My philosophy in selling is that customers deserve unbiased and honest advice on products and services. Anyone who misleads the buyers creates a very negative image for the company and himself, and loses credibility, which is one of the most precious attributes in business.

4.   **Have you ever done any foolish things?**
In your answer, stick to your childhood days. Give them an example from that period. Unless you are being interviewed for a position in a circus, tell them you haven't done any foolish things. You always think before you act and always assume full responsibility.

A: Although I don't mind an occasional laugh every now and then, I think there is no room for foolishness in the workplace. My attitude has always been one of maturity, reliability and professionalism. I always consider all pros and cons before taking action and avoid acting impulsively or immaturely.

Job motivation

1.   **Can you name a few things that motivate you in your job?**

A: I have always been self-motivated. I like that winning feeling when I do a good job, and the sense of achievement and job satisfaction motivates me to make even bigger efforts. I also like being around people who are capable, hard working and good team players. I enjoy interaction with my co-workers and team spirit.

2. **Tell me about an instance when you worked hard and felt proud of your achievement?**

This is a similar question to question 4 on page 111. You can use the same frame, with additional emphasis on factors that were additional sources of motivation in those instances.

3. **What were your reasons for leaving your last job?**

A: My last job was an interesting and creative one. It provided daily challenges and required hard work. Initially, I was learning a lot, but then I realised that I was specialising in a very narrow field and lacking skills and experience in other aspects of _____ (*sales, human resources, law*). I also realised that I would have to broaden my skills and experience to be able to handle the demands future developments may bring.

4. **What were the most important events or persons in your career development?**

A: My career development started during my school days. My _____ (*mathematics, arts, English*) teacher recognised my talents for _____ (*figures, drawing, literature*) and had a big influence on my choice of career by encouraging me to excel in that area. At university, my mentor helped me learn a lot about the subject and taught me many valuable lessons. In the work force, I had the privilege to work with and learn from a few brilliant _____ (*surgeons, solicitors, graphic artists*). The experience I gained during that period prepared me well for the challenges that lay ahead.

5. **Who was the best boss you ever worked for?**

The interviewer wants to know what type of person gets the most out of you and what type of people you like working with. Talking about people we like is very revealing. It tells them more about you than about those people! Another important aspect is having the opportunity to learn from your former boss. Someone who has never worked for a good boss has missed a lot by not having a model on how to be a good boss himself.

A: The best boss I worked with was fair and consistent. He expected a lot from me, but also gave a lot in return. He taught me many necessary skills and work methods and provided constant motivation and encouragement for my efforts.

He didn't dictate what had to be done and when, but rather left it for me to decide and even make some minor mistakes in the process. It was all part of his training. We always felt mutual respect and trust for each other, and remained good friends even after I left the company. I consider myself very fortunate to have had him by my side early in my career, as a supervisor, teacher and remarkable person. He served as a role model for me and helped me develop my own leadership and inter-personal skills.

6. **Describe the worst boss you ever worked for?**
   Slippery ground. Remember the rule 'Never badmouth your former employers'? Explain systematically what that person's problems were and make sure you emphasise that everybody felt the same, that it wasn't just you who had problems dealing with him/her. Mention the steps you took to improve the relationship between the two of you and the successful outcomes of your efforts (if any).

7. **Why did you choose this particular career?**
   A: My interest in _____ (*mention your field of work*) goes back to my school days. I displayed strong _____ (*list important skills needed on the job and in your profession*) skills and the decision to enter this profession came as a natural progression from that early interest. I regard this field as a challenging and an interesting one, with many demands and a lot of hard work, but also full of opportunities and rewards for a job well done. It suits my capabilities and career plans, and I would think twice before changing my career path.

8. **What areas of your job and career do you like most?**
   Frame your answer to suit the position for which you are being interviewed. If it's a job as a project engineer, emphasise your inclination towards design work, budget control, dealing with customers and consultants, etc. If the job involves sales, highlight your interest in contacting customers, travel, and so on.

9. **How would you describe the ideal company? The company you would like to work for?**
   It is relatively easy to define an ideal place of work, but make sure you include some characteristics of the company you are being interviewed

by in your answer. Some call it adulation, but I call it opportunity to score some important points. Consider the following introduction and then finish with some positive aspects of the interviewer's company:

A: The progressive company provides a challenging, stimulating and supporting atmosphere for its employees and their achievements. It's a safe place to work and it treats employees fairly. People enjoy working there and give their best to achieve the company's goals and targets.

10.   **How many hours a day do you work in your present job?**
Even if you work only eight hours a day, mention the occasional overtime, the work you take home with you, assignments away from home, and so on. Employers like people with a habit of doing more than they are paid for. It makes them feel good.

A: My normal working hours are from _____ (*eight to five, nine to six*), but I regularly work nine or ten hours a day and a few hours on Saturdays, owing to my workload.

Resilience

- *Quality or ability of quickly recovering the original state of mind or condition after being stressed, pushed to the limit, disappointed, mistreated, neglected, criticised or rejected, while maintaining effectiveness.*

1.   **Tell me about some of the biggest disappointments in your career and how you coped with them.**
A: I couldn't say that I have had any big disappointments in my career. I've been doing the type of work I like and that makes good use of my knowledge and experience. The only disappointing factor I've encountered so far is some people who don't share my enthusiasm and pride in hard work, and who don't have the drive needed to achieve targets and contribute to their employer's success.

Those people are more interested in their salaries and pay rises and it is hard to get any cooperation from them. I am not saying that everybody should share my values and views, but the unprofessional and laid back attitude has an impact on the work group and the whole department and its performance.

2. **Have you gained any benefits from your disappointments?**
*The message should be: You have learned a lot from your disappoint-
ments and mistakes. You never repeat the same mistake twice. You
always analyse what went wrong, when, how and why.*

A: I have learned a lot from mistakes, either my own or those of
others. I wouldn't call them disappointments, just temporary setbacks. Whenever I made a mistake my first task was to analyse
what went wrong and how it could have been prevented. That way I
never repeated mistakes and always anticipated potential problems.

3. **What career or business would you consider if you were
starting all over again?**
*There are two possible answers. If you are being interviewed for a job
in the same industry, you would choose the same career again. If you
are changing career, the answer will depend on the job you are
applying for. If you want to go into marketing, the answer should be:
marketing.*

A: If I had to choose my career again, I would make the same choice. I
feel happy and I think this profession suits me well. This is what I do
best, it is the area in which I can achieve my goals and make a
significant contribution to my employer.

4. **Have you ever been refused promotion or a pay rise?**
A: I have never had to ask for promotion or a payrise. My employers
recognised the value of my contribution and increased my salary
according to performance evaluations, which have always been
favourable.

5. **Are you sensitive to criticism?**
A: If the criticism is warranted, I try to analyse the problem, whatever
it is, and rectify it. If I feel that the criticism is unfair or without
grounds, I try to establish the reasoning behind it. If I feel that I'm
doing something right, I don't pay too much attention to unwar-
ranted criticism.

6. **We all feel frustrated or angry at times. Have you ever
resigned in frustration?**

Another knockout question. Tell them you walked out on a job and you will find yourself walking from the interview without a job.

A: No, I haven't. People who resign or give up when facing a problem or difficulty of any kind at work lack persistence and resilience. Whenever I had personal or work-related difficulties I resolved them successfully.

7. **If there was something about yourself that you would like to improve, what would it be?**

This is a knockout question, too, although a well-disguised one. Make sure you select some minor flaw or deficiency, the one that couldn't have a big impact on your chances to get a job. Paperwork is always a useful example, as are filing and record-keeping skills. You concentrate on how to achieve major targets and goals and in the process neglect the paperwork, but you finish it later. Some relatively harmless shortcomings like that would be good examples.

Stress management

1. **Under what working conditions do you produce your best results?**

A: Like any self-starter and achiever, I tend to produce the best results in the right work environment. By the right work environment I mean a harmonious one, where team members work together towards a common goal and concentrate their efforts to get the job done in the shortest possible time. Their intellectual and practical capabilities are challenged and put to the test, and some pressure is present. That gives them a sense of urgency of the job and stretches their faculties to the limit. They have all equipment necessary to do the job, and undivided support from their supervisor or manager. That is the environment in which people improve in their jobs and achieve tangible results.

2. **How well do you work under pressure?**

This is a leading question. The answer is obvious. You thrive under pressure. Everybody knows that nobody likes working under pressure, yet they still keep asking this question.

A: Working under pressure can be very productive. It can release untapped resources, such as inner strength and energy, and motivate people to excel themselves. I have worked under pressure quite often, owing to the nature of my vocation. This includes tasks that had to be done urgently, with limited resources, at short notice; in most cases I had to make decisions quickly and act on those decisions. I work quite well under pressure and I regard it as an additional motivator in the job.

3. **Have you ever lost your temper at work?**
   The same story again. You never lose your temper. You are patient, understanding, easy to deal with and everybody likes you a lot.

A: By maintaining an open and positive approach to problems and potential conflicts, I have managed to resolve occasional misunderstandings and disputes to the satisfaction of all parties. I work very well with my colleagues and never lose my temper. I regard that sort of behaviour as counterproductive and inappropriate. By losing your temper you cannot possibly resolve a problem – you can only make it worse.

4. **What kinds of pressure do you feel in your job?**
   Ability to work on urgent and demanding jobs, within budgetary constraints, at short notice, with limited resources, without sufficient information and with various types of people is highly regarded by employers. These are the pressures they are interested in.

A: There are various kinds of pressure in my job. The common one is when urgent and important jobs have to be done in minimum time, so production wouldn't suffer, or when goals and targets have to be achieved in a short time, within a limited budget or with a shortage of people. In most cases this kind of pressure provides motivation and tends to bring out the best in me.

5. **How do you relax after a hard day at work?**
   Your relaxation method should be perceived as active or semi-active. Don't just tell them that you hit the bed or sink into a recliner chair while watching a soap opera. Mention activities that project a constructive image and reflect high energy levels, such as walking, jogging, swimming, gardening, playing with the kids, etc.

6. **Would you classify yourself as a hard-driving or relatively laid back personality?**
    Naturally, you have to tell them that you're a hard working, no-nonsense achiever. In today's competitive climate, being laid back can not be viewed favourably.

A: When it comes to my job, I don't have time to be laid back. When I'm at work, I always give my best and try to achieve as much as possible. Of course, it is necessary to slow down from time to time to analyse my performance and plan future activities. Then, the hard driving starts again. I have always been self-motivated, and not to work hard would be against my personal beliefs.

Tenacity

*   *Staying with a position or sticking to a plan of action until the desired objective or final goal is achieved or no longer achievable within a reasonable time.*

Key words: persistence, commitment, perseverance, overcoming obstacles and problems.

1. **What were the biggest problems that you faced at university/college?**
A: I didn't have any problems at university. I enjoyed every minute of it, especially the constant interactions with people and the busy schedule. Some courses were difficult, but I worked hard and eventually succeeded.

2. **Tell me about some obstacles you had to overcome in the past.**
A: To achieve success in life and reach my goals I have had to put a lot of time and effort into overcoming obstacles such as _____ (*studying part time, learning a new language and adapting to a different culture, handling difficult people, the death of my wife/father/son*).

3. **Have you had an experience where you achieved your goal because you persisted for a length of time?**

A: To get my university degree I had to study hard for four/five years and pass more than forty exams. It required persistence, stamina and lots of hard work. All those efforts paid off, because now I am able to use my knowledge and experience at work. The main reason for my success is the fact that I had my goal clearly in my mind and that I had no doubts about the positive outcome. I believed in myself.

4.   **Sometimes we do our best, but fail to reach the target. Tell me about your experiences related to that situation.**
When answering this question make sure you emphasise that the cause for the failure wasn't you, but something else: unrealistic target, inadequate equipment or resources, short time . . .

A: I haven't had many failures of that kind in my career. The closest I got to it was during my involvement in a project when the project team faced a couple of problems such as _____ (*delays in equipment delivery, strikes/industrial actions, inadequate human resources, lack of funds*). Although I managed to carry out my task to the best of my abilities and achieve most of the targets, the project was delayed.

Work standards

●   *Positive traits: High personal standards, not satisfied with poor or average performance, high standards set for peers and subordinates and the whole organisation, meeting deadlines and demands of the job.*

1.   **How do you define doing a good job in your profession?**
This example is applicable to engineers, planners and supervisors in project management and control, but the format is similar for other professions.

A: The basic standard performance indicator in project management is completion of projects on time and within budget, while complying with the applicable standards and regulations, and in accordance with the project documentation (specifications, tenders, scope of work).

To me a good job means the one I'm proud of, that gives me a sense of achievement and internal satisfaction, and is in line with my professional reputation. A job well done is the one that sets new personal and organisational standards, serves as a reference or milestone for future similar undertakings and gives satisfaction and impeccable service to the end user, who is always the final judge of the product.

2. **There were probably some times when you were not satisfied with your performance. What have you done about it?**
    Whenever you tell them something that isn't 100 per cent positive about yourself, you have to follow up immediately and explain what steps you took to rectify the problem or improve your performance. This question is a typical example. The interviewer wants to hear that you can recognise a potential problem or a shortcoming and take adequate action to correct it.

3. **How often have you missed deadlines and what were the usual causes?**
A: I very rarely miss deadlines, owing to my planning and organising skills and general project management abilities. My experience plays an important role in anticipating the problems and prevention of the things that could go wrong. Good planning and effective control over the work force and equipment is the most effective weapon in the battle with time and mounting costs.

    Unexpected events, however, do occur, and that is the time for the revision of a plan and for urgent measures. On a few occasions the project I managed was late, mostly because of industrial action or unforeseen difficulties in sourcing and delivery of parts and equipment.

4. **Tell me about times when you were very pleased with the job you had done. Why did you feel that way?**
A: On quite a few occasions I have managed to achieve required _____ (*production targets, sales figures*) in much shorter time than planned and with a significant surplus in the budget. I was pleased with my delegation and work allocation methods, for they contributed significantly to the successful completion of tasks.

5. **Give me an example of times when your supervisor talked to you about your performance.**
The question doesn't specify poor performance, so use the opportunity to emphasise your favourable performance appraisals.

6. **How do you judge the performance of your staff? What are the differences between a good employee and an average one?**
This theoretical question calls for a classic answer. Read the section about 'ideal employees' and use the employer's views as your own. Even the worst employees know what 'good employee' means.

A: To judge the performance of others, one has first to establish the criteria that will be used in the process. Once those criteria are communicated to employees, they will know what aspects of their performance will be monitored. Some of my criteria include attendance records (punctuality, hours worked, number of sick days), successful completion of projects and tasks (on time and within budget), loyalty to the company, the ability to work well with others and continuous improvement of skills and performance. Good employees assume responsibility and take action when the job has to be done. They always work to the best of their abilities and can be trusted and relied upon in difficult times.

7. **Have you ever dismissed an employee for not performing adequately? What were the circumstances?**
A: I have recently fired an employee because of her poor performance. She couldn't adopt the company work standards, despite working to the best of her abilities. She wasn't suited for the position and the performance of the whole department suffered. After dismissal, she was hired by another department, and I believe she's doing a fine job there. That validated my opinion of her abilities and proved my feeling that she could be a valuable employee in a position that suits her talents and skills better.
or
So far I haven't been in a position to hire or fire people, but there were cases when my colleagues were dismissed because of poor attitude and poor performance, which were affecting the whole section.

8. **Are you satisfied with your department's and your company's performance in the last year or two?**
    Whenever you talk about your former or current place of employment, don't use 'they', use 'we'. That way you project loyalty to your employer, despite the fact that you are looking for another job. The interviewer will be assured that once you join their team you will be loyal to them. Anyone who says 'they' isn't, psychologically, working for his company.

A: Despite a harsh economic climate and widespread recession, the company maintained its position in the market, and even improved slightly. The introduction of enterprise bargaining and abolishment of restricted work practices resulted in improved overall efficiency and performance. The funds are still limited and more jobs are expected to go in near future. Overall, our performance last year could be described as adequate.

--------- **Interpersonal skills** ---------

Adaptability

> *It is the nature of a man as he grows older to protest against change, particularly change for the better.*
>
> John Steinbeck

- *Maintaining effectiveness and productivity in diverse environments and under the influence of various positive or negative factors.*
- *Accepting new ideas, work practices, policies and procedures.*
- *Adapting to different people, their methods of communication, work practices and management style.*

1. **From your résumé I see that you have changed jobs several times over the last few years, and some of the jobs were in the country. What problems have you had to face when moving?**

A: I have always enjoyed meeting new people and going to different places. So far I have been able to recognise the opportunities and therefore gain valuable experience working for diversified companies in various counties of Britain. Each move was different and none of them was easy, but the rewards and achievements always outweighed small inconveniences. My family shares my views and we haven't had any problems in moving house, making new friends, and adapting our lifestyle to suit local conditions.

2. **Generally speaking, there are some differences between working in privately owned companies and working in government departments. What do you think those differences are? Have you had any problems in adapting to one or the other?**
   There are two possible answers. Which one you are going to use will depend on the employer that is interviewing you. Don't praise the private sector when interviewing for a job in a government department and vice versa. Whichever the case, tell them that differences aren't major ones and you haven't had any problems in adapting to different working environments.

3. **Give me an example of a situation when you had to adjust quickly to changes in priorities or in the organisational structure. What was the impact of the change on you and how difficult was it to accept?**
   The best example here would be a situation when your boss was away and you performed his duties for a period of time. Mention the fact that you had to learn new skills quickly in order to meet the demands of the job, adjust to different priorities, supervise your co-workers and still do most of your normal duties.

4. **How do you manage to attend interviews while still employed?**
   The worst thing would be to say something like 'I told my employer I'm sick'. Your integrity would be damaged and you would lose many points for that.

A: I've taken a few days off from my unused last year's annual leave, to give myself enough time to schedule and attend interviews. Due to my workload that wasn't easy and some overtime and weekend work will be necessary to make up for it, but I'm used to working long hours. I try not to be absent from work for more than a few days at a time unless I am taking my annual holiday.

5. **What are your feelings about working for a large company like ours?**

Nobody really likes large-scale organisation; nobody likes to take orders from a superior who takes orders from a superior who takes orders . . .

E F Schumacher, *Small is Beautiful*

Beware of the hierarchy, bureaucracy and constraints of most big companies. In your answer, reflect on positive aspects and don't mention the negatives.

A: I would welcome the opportunity to work in a large, reputable firm such as this. The strength, market position and resources of such a well-established organisation are not available in smaller companies. That strong base presents a foundation for achievement and potential for advancement and diversification.

6. **What is your attitude towards working in a small company such as this one?**

Big companies are small companies that succeeded.

Robert Townsend, *Up The Organisation*

A: Most innovative, energetic and highly competitive companies are not big in size. I have always valued highly the participation of employees in the decision-making process and 'the family feeling' of the small company, where team spirit, daily challenges and hands-on involvement in solving business problems bring a sense of achievement and a quick response to changes and new opportunities.

Assertiveness

- *Having or showing confidence in oneself, belief and trust in one's own powers.*
- *Being firm and direct in conversation.*
- *The ability to stand up for one's beliefs and rights.*

Most interviewers don't ask questions on assertiveness. The whole interview can give them a very good idea of how assertive you are. However, it is still possible that you may be asked one of the following questions:

1. **Do you make your opinion known if your point of view differs from that of your superiors?**

   In the 'back-covering' process, most of us voice our opinions if we don't share our superiors' ideas. If you agree to do something you don't want to be held liable for, you had better tell them so. That way the responsibility will lie on someone else's shoulders. Use something along these lines, but don't mention shedding the responsibility. The interviewer is testing your assertiveness and independence. Tell him you always speak up and try to discuss issues with your boss so you can come up with a mutually acceptable solution.

   A: I always discuss issues and problems with my superiors. If my point of view differs from theirs, I put myself into their shoes and try to see it. Then I explain my opinions to them. In that process the right solution is almost always found.

2. **If you had to characterise yourself in one sentence, what would you say?**

   Some interviewers like this sort of trap question. You have two options. Try to summarise on your strongest points or offer a 'no-answer' reply.

   A: My main assets are the ability to communicate effectively and work individually or in a team, set goals and achieve them, and get the required jobs done (*good answer*).
   or
   I don't think you would like to hire anybody who can characterise himself in one sentence (*even better*).

3.   **Give me an example of some of the most difficult one-to-one discussions or meetings you have had with your colleagues or subordinates?**
A good example that could be used here is the occasion when you had to fire someone. If you have done that in the past, use it to score a few points by presenting yourself as considerate, tactful and compassionate, but also as a firm, no nonsense decision maker and action taker.

A: Some performance evaluation discussions and especially termination discussions were the most difficult for me. Certain people find it very hard to assume responsibility and accountability for their actions. That called for special skills in handling those meetings. I always try to put myself in other people's perspective, but I also make sure that they understand my point of view by being firm and resisting the intimidation and bullying tactics some of them use.

Behavioural flexibility

- *The ability to change and adjust views, methods used and behaviour, to suit the particular situation or task.*
- *The capability to accept change around you.*

1.   **Describe for me an occasion when, after your initial proposal or idea was rejected, you used a different approach and achieved your goal. What was the difference between the two approaches?**

A: At my job with _____ (*the name of your employer*) one of my proposals for purchasing some advanced equipment used for _____ purposes was rejected due to insufficient capital funds at the time. I didn't give up. My following strategy was simple, but it proved effective. I clearly stated the problem we had, listed annual figures that had been wasted and calculated anticipated savings that use of the proposed equipment would generate. I re-presented my request using graphs, charts and tables, and the management liked the new proposal and the whole idea!

2. **Have you had any experience in supervising people with advanced degrees? Did you use a different approach to establish rapport with those individuals?**

A: My job with _____ (*name a previous employer*) required supervision and coordination of technical staff, most of whom were engineers and scientists with higher degrees. It was a great opportunity for me to learn from those professionals, and the whole experience was very stimulating.

I enjoyed working with highly educated people. The most important aspect in building rapport with them was mutual respect and understanding of each other's needs and work philosophy. They have specific demands and need specific motivation and recognition for their work, of which they are very proud. Those traits did require slightly different supervision methods.

3. **How do you feel about a formal dress code in our department?**

Some companies have strict dress codes, such as a shirt, a tie and a jacket for men (no jeans or casuals) and a dress or skirt for women (no trousers). Tell them you would wear whatever is required by the code.

A: The dress code in your department/company suits me. I have always liked to dress formally and feel very comfortable wearing suits. I realise that a standard of dress is necessary for a company in this business in order to project a positive image to its customers and the general public.

4. **How would you feel about working for a female supervisor?**

A: I have worked very successfully with female managers and supervisors before. I don't differentiate between people on the basis of their gender, the only thing that matters to me is their personality, efficiency and professionalism.

5. **Have you ever worked for a boss younger or less experienced than yourself?**

A: I haven't worked for such a boss. My former bosses were mostly very experienced professionals from whom I've learned a lot. In a sense, they were role-models for me.

or

A: I have worked for a younger boss before. He was a good manager and motivator, we had a very productive relationship and got along really well. I don't consider age so important, what matters is a person's credibility, professionalism and competency.

6. How important to you is the aim to build relationships with clients, co-workers, peers or management?

A: To me, interactions between people are the most important factor in any business. The ability to work together as a team, absolute honesty with peers and customers, and a mutual feeling of trust and understanding, are essential for creating an efficient environment.

A good team is always greater than the sum of the individual values of its members. A new dimension is created when people work harmoniously together.

7. What types of people annoy you?

A: People who annoy me are those who are not prepared to do their best at work and contribute as team members. Unprofessional, unethical, dishonest people, gossipers and backstabbers are equally destructive and annoying. I find it hard to trust them and rely on them. Usually, all those people are interested in are their pay cheques.

Independence

- *Taking action in your own hands.*
- *Resisting the influence of others.*
- *Making your views known.*
- *Being a self-starter, recognising problems and taking actions to rectify them.*
- *The ability to work alone, with minimal supervision or without direct supervision.*

1. What kinds of decisions do you make independently in your present job? Give me some examples of those decisions.

A: In my job as ____, I'm responsible for all issues related to ____. Since I work alone most of the time, or as part of a small team, I have to make various kinds of decisions regularly and independently. For example, I decide ____.

2. **Tell me about an instance when you took a matter in your hands although it should have been handled by your superiors.**
   This is a good opportunity to demonstrate your ability to handle more complex problems successfully and get the jobs done. In addition to that, your initiative and tendency to assume higher responsibilities and take calculated risks can be illustrated.

3. **Do you prefer working alone or being part of a team?**
   The answer to this question would have to be tailored to suit the nature of the job you are being interviewed for. No matter which style of work prevails, don't forget to mention that you work effectively in any case.

   A: Owing to the nature of my occupation and the kind of tasks that I encounter in my job, I have worked independently for a number of years. The broad range of my skills, my knowledge of the subject and my systematic and organised approach to work, make me self-dependent and efficient in meeting the demands of this profession. I have also worked as part of a team where I had the opportunity to learn from others and improve my teamwork skills.
   or
   Although I have worked alone before, I prefer team spirit and the interactions between team members while working towards a common goal. In a team people learn from each other and tend to achieve results faster, more efficiently and with greater satisfaction. The team approach to problem solving creates a homogenous work force and a more productive environment.

4. **Have you ever worked alone, without any supervision at all?**
   Most people have worked without direct supervision or any supervision at all. Exploit the fact that you successfully completed the tasks given to you and that you didn't need any help or assistance. Mention

your systematic approach to problem solving, the use of experience gained in similar situations and the ability to identify and rectify problems.

A: I have worked without supervision for prolonged periods of time. As a self-starter I can identify problems, devise a plan of action and assume full responsibility for my activities and the successful completion of required tasks.

5. Do you consider yourself to be a self-starter?

A: I do consider myself a self-starter. I never rely on someone else's initiative, I take the initiative myself. My education and experience have enabled me to be able to recognise potential problems and areas critical to the successful accomplishment of projects. Trend watching and looking for clues are important in the process.

6. What do you do in your job that is not covered by your job description? Why do you do that type of work?

A: To achieve goals and produce results I sometimes choose to perform various tasks that are not, strictly speaking, a part of my job. Modern work practices and a competitive climate call for more flexibility and a broader range of skills. By doing more than required I not only learn more, I also become more efficient and productive. If I'm able to do the task, instead of waiting for the job to be done, I simply do it.

7. Have you ever felt the company's constraints on you and have you ever had to go against those traditions and policies to reach your goal?

Similar to question 2 on page 128. It's a Catch-22 situation: by displaying your initiative and independence you go against the rules; if you always play by the rules you will not be seen as innovative. Between two evils choose the lesser one.

A: We all feel the constraints of some policies and procedures from time to time. However, to achieve uniformity and consistency and to ensure that relevant standards and regulations are followed, it is necessary to have those policies and procedures in place. It is always possible to 'cut corners' and achieve the required results sooner or with less effort, but I have never taken the path of least resistance.

Negotiation skills

1. **Have you had experience in negotiating big deals with suppliers? What have you achieved as the outcome of those negotiations?**

A: My experience in negotiation helped me get some very good deals on spare parts and equipment for projects. I had established a very good and professional relationship with vendors and suppliers, so getting the best price possible was the natural outcome of my efforts. On average, I achieved savings of between ten and twenty per cent on listed wholesale prices, and in some cases discounts were as high as forty per cent. Some vendors and retailers are very keen to establish a business with big companies and subsequent price reductions could be significant.

2. **Tell me about an instance when you had to negotiate with union officials about an issue that could not be resolved 'by the book'.**

A: In one instance I was involved in negotiations regarding the use of _____ (*mention the situation from your experience*). It was a specific issue and union officials were not to keen to accept the changes, but after long, hard negotiations and confrontations they agreed, and the changes were implemented successfully.

3. **When you applied for your previous jobs, did you negotiate your salary or did you simply accept the figures determined by the employers?**

   Apart from evaluating your negotiation skills, this question probes into a sensitive area of salary negotiations. Whatever you say may be used against you when the time comes to talk about money. So, use extreme caution here!

A: Because of my education, knowledge and relevant professional experience, I was always able to negotiate better terms of my employment with employers, who realised that money-saving measures could not attract high calibre candidates, and that any additional money conceded would be the best investment possible – the investment in the right person for the job!

4. **Have you ever had to negotiate terms of a contract with a customer in order to get a sale? What concessions did you make and what was the outcome?**

A: In today's buyer's market it is sometimes necessary to negotiate the price of a contract or some of the terms in order to get a sale. I have had a few cases of that kind.

    Although I made a few small concessions in response to customers' growing demands, I managed to change other aspects of those contracts. Those gains brought additional revenue from the customers, without them realising it. Tough negotiation is not always the best approach to securing deals. Sometimes 'don't change the price, change the package' tactics work much better.

Sales ability/persuasiveness

> *Two shoe salesmen find themselves in a rustic, backward part of Africa. The first salesman wires back to his head office: 'There is no prospect of sales. No one wears shoes here'. The other salesman wires: 'No one wears shoes here. We can dominate the market. Send all possible stock'.*
>
> William Davis, *The Innovators*

1. **What are the best ideas/suggestions/proposals you made to your boss? How successful were they?**
    When answering this question, select an instance when your proposal was accepted. Make sure you outline the benefits to your employer that resulted from your contributions.

2. **Explain briefly your attitude and approach to selling either products or ideas. What methods do you use and why?**

A: My whole approach to selling is based on the fact that whenever we want to get cooperation from people, persuade them to buy something or win an argument, we have to speak in other person's terms.

For example, instead of urging the customers to buy equipment or products that I think they need, I encourage them to give me their ideas. That way customers feel they are coming up with ideas, creating the designs and making decisions. Once I succeed in doing this, I don't have to sell. They buy.

3. **Describe for me your most satisfying experience in gaining management support for your idea or proposal.**
   This question requires a specific example from your past experience. Select an instance when you achieved savings, increased profits, improved safety or work practices or initiated something significant.

A: Based on my experience in logistics, warehouse management and stock control, I devised a program for the reduction of the number of spare parts kept on the shelf and better stock management generally. The program was relatively easy to implement and resulted in considerable savings. The management welcomed the idea and recognised my efforts by promoting me to the position of Warehouse Supervisor.

4. **What was your most disappointing experience in attempting to persuade your superiors to accept your views?**

A: My opinions and views are generally highly regarded and sought after by management, owing to my knowledge of the job and relevant experience. There were, however, a couple of occasions when decisions were made despite my strong objections. In one instance, some important earthmoving equipment was overdue for a major service, but it was decided to postpone the service for a considerable period. The equipment failed catastrophically, as I predicted, and expenses were high.

5. **What do your subordinates think your strengths and weaknesses are? How do you know they would respond that way?**

A: It's a bit difficult to predict their response to this question. Judging by my successful and professional relationship with them, I would expect to be portrayed as a fair and firm leader, good communicator and a person of high integrity and morale. I have always been able to motivate them, even when times were tough and tasks demanding.

———— Communication skills ————

1.   How do you assure your subordinates and co-workers that you are listening to what they say?

A: When I make a decision or take action that involves my co-workers or subordinates, I always make sure I get their input. It is important to adapt to different personality styles and get constant feedback in order to avoid conflicts, misunderstandings or bad feelings. The doors of my office are open to people with constructive suggestions, work-related problems and genuine enquiries.

2.   Have you ever misinterpreted any instruction, message or information? What were the outcomes of those situations?

A: I always devote my exclusive attention to the person speaking to me. That way most misunderstandings can be eliminated and effective communication established. I notice that most poor listeners, when they are not talking, are busy rehearsing what they are going to say next. That way it is very difficult to exchange ideas and messages.

3.   Have you ever done any public speaking or presentations?

A: Owing to the nature of my profession, presentations, meetings and conferences play a very important role in my day-to-day activities. As part of _____ (*an award restructuring, a company's ongoing educational policy, etc.*) I run a few training courses for _____ (*tradesmen, clerical staff, trainees*).

So far I have successfully participated in various seminars, presentations and conferences and delivered speeches on a wide range of _____ (*technical, managerial, scientific*) topics.

4.   What were some of the biggest or most demanding groups/ audiences you made presentations to?

A: Last year I participated in _____ (*The Third International Conference on Molecular Biology, Electrical Energy Symposium, etc.*) My research paper was published and I was one of the speakers. The participants and guests were very prominent _____ (*scientists,* *engineers, managers*), specialising in that area. Judging by the number of questions I had to answer after the speech, my presentation was well received.

5.   **Have you ever written any procedures, specifications, policies, tenders or similar documents for use by a client or your own firm?**

A: Writing equipment specifications/tenders/operational procedures is a vital part of my role as _____ (*project engineer, operations foreman, construction superintendent*). That kind of technical document ensures that equipment and services provided by my company meet all relevant standards and any additional predetermined criteria. Likewise, any contract, service or equipment provided by vendors has to comply with our specifications and internal standards.

6.   **What types of written proposals or reports have you done?**

A: My present position includes the writing of _____ (*give details*) reports and proposals. Each of the document types mentioned requires a different approach and makes use of different writing techniques to convey the message in the most effective way.

7.   **What were some of your most difficult writing assignments?**

A: I have written quite a few important and very demanding writing assignments, but the most challenging one was my _____ (*Diploma/Masters/PhD Thesis*). The hard work and time invested in its preparation paid off, for it received very favourable reviews and was awarded the highest distinction.

8.   **Have you ever had to write technical/training manuals for _____ (tradespeople, plant operators, catering staff, etc)?**

A: So far I haven't been involved in that type of activity, but part of my duty is to _____ (*revise and update operating procedures regularly, produce short instructions to line people, implement communication plans and strategies*). I feel confident in my technical writing abilities and if this job requires that, it shouldn't take me long to produce top quality documents.

or

A: While with _____, I produced a comprehensive training manual for the training of _____ (*salesmen, crane operators, nurses, boiler makers*). I also wrote a few chapters in the company's Internal Procedures Manual.

9. What are the most important documents/proposals/ reports you have ever written?

A: Most of my business proposals and tenders were successful, even at times of recession and in the highest sectors of the market, but the _____ (*£400,000, £1 million, . . .*) tender for _____ project made the most significant contribution to my employer's profitability in the past year. I devoted a great deal of my energy and experience to that deal. My efforts were recognised and that gave me the greatest sense of achievement in my job at _____ Company.

10. Do you have any rules that you follow when writing reports/proposals? What are they? How do you implement them? Why are they important?
This is a typical example of multiple questions asked together. Make sure you remember all of them. If you don't, ask the interviewer to repeat the question(s). You don't have to answer them as if they were separate questions, but reflect on each of them in your answer.

A: There are some basic rules that have to be followed in writing. First you have to determine what type of audience will read your written message. That fact will have an impact on the style and document format used. Secondly, you have to establish the purpose of the written assignment: what is the message for the readers? The next question to be considered is what aspects/points/details should be emphasised in order to achieve the goal of effective, clear and comprehensive communication. Finally, you come to the actual content of your written document. It should always include the three essential parts: an introduction, a body and a conclusion. That format is usually the most effective way to get the message and information to the readers.

──────── Management ability ────────

Be prepared for some 'theoretical' questions here. Although most interviewers look for specific, action or problem orientated answers, and ask exact and precise questions to elicit such answers, some of them like broad general questions. The candidates' answers to these questions reveal a lot, not only what they say and are prepared to say, but also what they don't want to, or cannot, say! So, take a few hours to think about general topics such as management, the role of people in organisations, motivation, effective communication methods, and so on. It will help you express your views and better understand the interviewer's. Some of the typical questions of a general nature:

1. How would you define your management philosophy?

2. What do you think good management is?

3. What is your human resources philosophy? How would you define the role of people in the organisation?

Control

Ready? Shoot! Aim!

Japanese view of Western management techniques

1. **Describe a particularly difficult management situation you have encountered, how you approached the problem and the outcome of the whole situation.**
   Don't forget that the control methods you use and your control skills are being evaluated here. The core of your message should be that you were in control of events and people, not vice versa.

2. **What methods do you use to predict the future workload for your staff?**

A: The departmental monthly and yearly plans are the basis for predictions of that kind. Most major activities are scheduled (except breakdowns and equipment failures) and regularly updated and revised. Another important aspect of the planning process is previous experience and knowledge of the department and most factors that could have impact on the smooth running of the business.

(Now add some specific methods that you use or are planning to use.) The next two questions do not have listed answers. Many books have been written on subjects like Management By Objectives (MBO) and Total Quality Control (TQC). More and more managers are using these methods and the chances that you may be asked this type of question are increasing. However, opinions differ, although the positive ones are prevalent.

In your answers (if you have had experience with methods mentioned) concentrate on the benefits achieved, or, if you haven't had such experience, tell them you are familiar with the concepts and that you are considering implementing them. Then give reasons for your decisions or opinions regarding the effectiveness of advanced management methods.

3. **Do you use Management By Objectives (MBO)? How would you evaluate its effectiveness?**

4. **Are you familiar with Total Quality Control (TQC) concepts? Have you ever used or implemented TQC in your area of responsibility?**

Delegation

Make sure that you emphasise the fact that when you delegate tasks, you still have responsibility for the job being well done. Employers don't like people who shed or delegate their responsibility and accountability.

1. **Have you ever delegated responsibility?**
A: I make delegating tasks and responsibilities my constant goal. If you expect people to develop their skills and abilities, you have to give them responsibility. My method is to tell them what the objectives of a certain task are, what criteria will be used to evaluate their performance and then let them do it. I make myself available to help them along the way and to monitor their progress.

2.   What type of assignments do you delegate to your subordinates?

A: When I delegate a task or assign responsibility to a person, I have a very good idea of that employee's capabilities, strengths and weaknesses. To challenge and motivate people, I try to assign them tasks which are slightly above their current level of expertise. That way they keep learning and growing in the job. Sometimes it takes them a little longer to complete the assignments, but the benefits this approach brings are far greater than the drawbacks.

3.   What steps do you take in delegating?

A: First, I tell them what they are expected to accomplish, second, I set the standards they are expected to reach and third, I keep monitoring their progress and helping them if necessary. I make it my first priority to ensure the employees know how to handle a task and how to accomplish the goal.

4.   Have you ever made a mistake in delegating? Tell me about the outcome and what caused that mistake?

A: I couldn't say I made mistakes in delegating, but I had some temporary setbacks when I delegated tasks that were far above the capabilities of my subordinates. The initial results were not as good as they could have been, but in the long run the benefits were obvious, for my subordinates acquired new skills and mastered demanding tasks.

Initially, when I started the job, I wasn't delegating enough, mostly due to the fact that I didn't know my workers well. Once I learned their capabilities, I gained confidence in them and became successful in delegating. That's what delegating is all about: confidence in people.

5.   How do you keep track of assignments made to subordinates?

A: I use a simple but effective computerised filing system. Each employee has an individual database file with all planned activities, estimated time schedule and information on progress and results achieved. That way I know what each person is doing at any time.

6. **Do you sometimes feel that to get a job done properly you have to do it yourself?**

A: People who feel that way don't have trust in their co-workers and subordinates and probably don't know how to delegate properly. By knowing my people, their skills, abilities and personalities, I have been able to delegate tasks successfully and improve their skills.

7. **What kinds of decisions do you reserve for yourself? Why don't you delegate them to others?**

A: An effective manager doesn't delegate all his work. Some tasks are either too complex, too urgent or too important to be delegated. A manager should attend to those issues himself. Whenever a decision directly affects _____ (*people in my department, the company's profitability, legal issues, efficiency*) I make that decision and assume responsibility.

Developing subordinates

1. **Have you ever been involved in hiring employees?**

A: So far I haven't been in the position to make decisions on hiring, but I have been involved in the evaluation of applicants and in making recommendations and giving expert advice on their suitability and level of technical knowledge.

or

As a _____ (*supervisor, department manager*) I have interviewed candidates for various positions within the company. Either individually or as a member of a recruiting panel, I have been involved in the selection and hiring of the best applicants.

2. **How do you help your subordinates to improve their performance?**

A: In my opinion, the best motivator and the best help in the learning process is personal attention. I always make myself available to people by creating a supportive and productive atmosphere which will encourage them to learn, improve and expand their views. That sort of atmosphere helps them build confidence in themselves, in the company and in their manager.

3. **What is your opinion of the importance of training and development?**

A: In today's rapidly changing business climate, effective training is absolutely necessary in order to improve efficiency and readiness of the work force. However, training is not just about developing skills. It is an instrument for attaining the company's objectives such as innovation, creative thinking, workers' participation in decision making and total quality control. Training and development is about human resources and their role in the productive environment.

4. **What are the major training and development needs of the people in your department?**

A: The training needs in my department vary not only between certain groups of people, but also between individuals. (*Give details.*) Also, there is training in supervision and management methods for senior professionals, supervisors and managers. Some members of our team are currently studying for their post-graduate degrees.

5. **What management methods and techniques do you use in developing your staff?**

A: In the area of human resource developments, I have initiated and put into practice a few programs. Our annual performance review analyses accomplishments and areas for improvement, and serves as a basis for determining the skills that each particular employee is lacking. The Human Resources Review, which also takes place once a year, outlines the specific steps employees should take in order to improve their skills and acquire new knowledge.

Last, but not least, through daily contacts with my subordinates, I keep aware of their talents, strengths and weaknesses, and ask for their views on their own training and development needs.

6. **What is your attitude towards human resources philosophy and the role of people in today's organisations?**

A: It sounds like a cliché, but people are the company's most important asset. It can't be seen directly on balance sheets and annual reports, but people are the key to peak performance and, subsequently, business success. It today's work force, which is more educated and skilled than ever before, the task of every manager and supervisor is to establish communication channels, allow free flow of information and implement the programs and policies which will motivate people, prepare them for challenges and give them job satisfaction, which is perceived as increasingly important for creating the right business climate.

Leadership

To lead people, walk behind them.

Lao-Tzu

The Western world has been suffering from a chronic lack of leaders for quite some time. A majority of companies suffers from that illness, too. These days, most employees are administered. They are treated as numbers, not people. Rules and regulations don't leave much room for leadership. Policies are inflexible and the companies apply them across the board. In such a climate, it is very difficult to nurture leadership.

Leadership is closely associated with innovation, vision and trust. Sadly, you won't find too much of that in many of today's organisations. However, some employers value leadership more than others and it is likely that they may ask you one or more of the following questions to assess your leadership abilities.

1.   Do you think you are a smart person?

A: To me, smart people are not necessarily the ones with high IQs. Education and intelligence is the ability to meet life's situations and perform in the job to the best of one's abilities. We show our value by the way we deal with people, approach business problems and make decisions.

With that in mind and without any false modesty I would consider myself a smart person. Of course, there are many things I don't know, but I make constant learning and self-improvement my main goal. To me, to be smart means to ask questions, listen to what people say, apply knowledge and know-how to problems and learn from my own and, preferably, from other people's mistakes.

2. Do you like working with people?

The ability to be a contributing member of a team by dealing successfully with people from various backgrounds is viewed as essential by employers.

A: I have always enjoyed the teamwork and interaction with my co-workers and customers. In today's very competitive and highly specialised business environment, it is of paramount importance to organise and coordinate the efforts of many people in order to achieve goals and sustain growth. Although I consider my ability to work well with people, to motivate them and communicate with them effectively one of the my most important assets, I try constantly to keep improving those skills even further.

3. How do you show interest and keep in contact with your co-workers?

A: The key to successful people handling lies in knowing them. So I make sure I have a good idea about what they want, what their feelings are and what they expect from me. Showing them what my ideas can do for them makes them more receptive and cooperative. I show interest through regular meetings, discussions and consultations with them, and through becoming genuinely interested in their work and achievements.

4. In your opinion, what makes a good manager?

A: Good managers are people dedicated to company goals and policies, people who know how to manage employees, motivate them and develop them to their fullest potential. The good manager creates the right kind of environment by stimulating the desire to excel in his/her employees, delegating responsibility and promoting teamwork.

5. What, specifically, do you do to set an example for your subordinates/co-workers?

A: My personal credo is not to ask anything from my subordinates that I, as manager, wouldn't ask from myself. To be fair and just, to treat people with respect and to be genuinely interested in them, are the secrets of my success. I consider creating the right work environment my most important task, and to achieve that, I have to start with myself, by setting the right example for my workers.

6. **What was the most difficult group you had to cooperate with? Why was dealing with them difficult?**

The answer to this question will depend on your particular occupation and experience. You can refer to a problem with a demanding, unprofessional, unethical, unmotivated, abusive or uncooperative client, another department, work group, contractor or any other group you had a problem dealing with.

Whichever example you use, make sure you emphasise the steps you took to rectify the problem, your efforts and willingness to resolve the issue. A good example would be handling an industrial dispute or strike (after it happened) or discussions and negotiations with workers and union officials in order to prevent it from happening. Companies with strong anti-union sentiments would love your tough approach and loyalty to your employer.

7. **Do you have any staff who do not work together well? What have you done to rectify the problem?**

A: Most of my staff work together very well and have strong feelings of belonging to the team. Occasionally, there are some misunderstandings and disputes that have to be resolved, but that's more of an exception than a rule. My task in those cases is to act as a mediator, bringing people together and openly discussing the issues. It is very important for me to preserve neutrality, maintain integrity and project sincerity in those circumstances.

8. **How would you define the difference between management and leadership?**

A: It isn't easy to define leadership. I see it as one of the managerial activities, the one which improves productivity by stimulating creativity, improving morale and personal satisfaction, influencing workers and redirecting their behaviour to satisfy a wide range of objectives.

Management, on the other hand, is about controlling the company's resources, making decisions that will increase efficiency and profitability, improving working conditions and safety, and creating a stable, reliable and motivated work force. Managers' tasks are to make sure the company's policies and procedures are adhered to, and to plan and control various activities which have to lead to desired results. To me, management is the issue of ability and controlling, while leadership is about trust, credibility and vision.

9. **Do you consider yourself a better manager or a better leader? What are the reasons for that?**

A: To be a good manager, you have to be familiar with company rules and policies, various legal issues, business methods and strategies, and planning and controlling process. Good leaders don't necessarily have those traits. Their biggest strength is their ability to lead and motivate people. They enjoy almost unquestioned support from their followers.

So far I have been able to achieve balance between those qualities, to be successful in a management process and to motivate people to achieve better results.

10. **How would you describe your job as a supervisor?**

A: The effective supervisor must perform certain functions to enable his team to carry out its tasks. He has to define tasks to be done, make a plan of how to achieve those tasks, allocate work and resources to individuals, control quality of work done and progression of jobs, constantly assess the performance against the plan and developed criteria, and adjust the plan, if necessary, to reflect changes and modifications. The supervisor also has to create an environment which will support the efforts of his team and make people more receptive to ideas, more enthusiastic about their work, loyal to their supervisor and the company and committed to the company's goals.

Planning, organising and time management

Work expands so as to fill the time available for its completion.

C. Northcote Parkinson

1. **What methods do you use in scheduling your time and setting priorities?**

A: I regard planning as an important tool in managing my work and achieving first-class results. I plan my time on daily, weekly, monthly and six-monthly bases. Software packages for scheduling and project management help me to adjust my plans and reschedule activities. These plans are the basis for daily 'to do' lists. Every evening I list issues and tasks to be performed the next day and assign priorities to them. My experience in carrying out the tasks of my job helps me determine those priorities.

2. **What action do you take when your plans and schedules are upset by unforeseen circumstances?**

A: A good plan, be it daily, weekly, monthly, or a longer range one, should always leave some room for unforeseen circumstances, problems or developments that are difficult or impossible to predict. When I plan or schedule activities, I try to build in a degree of flexibility and adaptability, so the eventual changes and rearrangements can be done quickly and easily, with minimum delays or interruptions of any kind. A reasonable contingency factor is imperative in uncertain or unstable times in some activities.

3. **What were your last year's objectives? Have you achieved them?**

   When talking about your plans and objectives, state not only what was planned, but also why, and how the plan was realised.

4. **How do you plan your day-to-day activities?**

A: My first job every morning is to go through my 'to do' list (created the day before, or during my previous weekly planning exercise), revise it and set priorities. Some jobs may be urgent and important, some may be important but not urgent and vice versa. To avoid procrastination I first attend to the tasks I dread most. Once I finish those tasks I feel much more confident and efficient, because I know that they have been accomplished.

5. **Who schedules your sales trips? How do you decide which clients to see and when?**

   Ideally, you should schedule your own trips. By telling them that, you project an image of an independent and organised decision maker.

A: My monthly, six-monthly and yearly plans serve as a basis for scheduling trips. Every now and then they have to be upgraded or changed owing to various developments, such as new projects starting, major upgrades of plants and equipment, unplanned purchases and changes in a client's personnel. All those events call for earlier visits and further building of business relationships. I make most decisions and plans myself, which are then approved by the Sales Manager.

6. **How do you familiarise yourself with the latest developments in your company after being away for a few days?**

A: When I'm away on business, I keep in touch with my superiors and my colleagues. Daily telephone contacts are very important for the smooth operation of the business. When I return, I spend a few minutes with each of the people I work with and review the developments that took place while I was away.

7. **Do you have a work backlog in your department? What factors caused that backlog?**

Never admit that you are the cause of the backlog. Even if you recognise the existence of a backlog in your department, you can emphasise that your projects/jobs/tasks are being completed on time or ahead of schedule. Underline the importance of your planning techniques.

8. **Do you use any software packages for project management? Why did you choose that particular program?**

A: I am familiar with a few project management programs, such as _____ (*Timeline, Project Manager Workbench, Harvard Project Manager, Microsoft Project,* . . .). I prefer _____, because of its capabilities and user friendliness. The manuals are comprehensive and well written and the technical support is outstanding.

9. **How do you keep a record of items and issues that require your attention? How do you prioritise them?**

A: I consider record keeping an important management tool. I use a diary to record all issues and events, as well as the whiteboard, for issues that I have to be aware of constantly. I also use daily 'to do' lists and 'people to see or call lists' which help me to organise and plan my time. A few levels of priority are assigned to various tasks and issues. Some of them may be important and urgent, urgent but not important, important but not urgent, and so on. Each priority reflects these criteria: importance and urgency.

10. **Describe a typical day in your job** *(if the candidate is employed).*
or
Describe a typical day on your last job *(for unemployed).*
Among other things, your skills in planning and organising your time, prioritising and scheduling your duties and managing your resources, are evaluated by this question. Efficiency, effective time management and organised approach to activities can help you frame your answer.

11. **Do you consider yourself a future-, present- or past-orientated person?**
A: I try to live in the present, thinking in terms of what needs to be done now, instead of thinking about the past or worrying about the future. The past experiences are always valuable, and making plans for the future is an important business activity, but I endeavour to concentrate my efforts on current problems and issues.

Staff coordination

1.. **What performance appraisal procedure and technique do you use for evaluating your subordinates?**
A: We have a formal six-monthly performance evaluation program, in a form of one-on-one discussions between the manager and each staff member. There is a detailed evaluation criteria that addresses attendance records, quality of work, ideas and suggestions made, training and development, achievement of goals and targets set on previous sessions, and so on. In addition to these formal evaluations, I use every opportunity to praise my staff for their efforts and recognise a job well done, or, if necessary, to reprimand them for poor performance, a discipline problem, or any serious breach of regulation or company policy.

2. How do you establish rapport with your staff and peers?

A: To me, establishing rapport seems to be a natural tendency. The greatest part is often established non-verbally. By being empathetic, treating people with respect and being willing to listen and help, I create a feeling of trust and confidence in my staff. Matching our behaviour to suit the particular situation or person also helps in a process. Matching voice tone or tempo to that of the person I'm talking to, controlling body language, posture and gesture is also important. All that is done almost automatically, naturally. I consider myself lucky for not having any problems in establishing rapport with my peers, superiors or staff.

3. Describe the basic form and content of your staff meetings.

A: Our daily meetings are very brief. They cover major tasks to be performed during the day, current developments and actualities. Weekly meetings communicate information from management and other departments, and include a planning session for the coming week. Each staff member gets a chance to contribute by informing others on his/her projects and activities, or by raising various issues or concerns. The chairpersons change on rotational basis. The manager acts as a mediator, moderator and coordinator.

4. To what extent do your subordinates participate in the decisions you make?

A: Whenever appropriate I ask for input from my colleagues and subordinates, either as an opinion or a recommendation. By involving them in the decision-making process, they feel active participants, not just passive bystanders with no say in the process. It also prepares them for more senior positions in the future. In some cases, team members make their own decisions and assume responsibility for the successful completion of a task.

5. Can you tell me about an instance when an employee came to you with a personal problem? How did you handle that situation?

A: I can recall quite a few of those instances. On one occasion, I noticed decreased productivity from one of my employees. The person I'm talking about was one of the best and most reliable workers, yet her performance was suffering for some reason. Just when I planned to talk to her, she came to see me and explained her problem. Her father was seriously ill in Europe and she asked me for a few days off, since she had used her annual leave a few months before. I checked the validity of her claims and approved ten days of paid leave on compassionate grounds. Everything ended well, her father recovered and she is still one of the best performers, more committed than ever.

6.   What actions do you take if your subordinate is not performing well in the job?

A: The first step in coaching the failing employee is to determine the causes for failure, such as lack of talent, lack of motivation or interest, inexperience, inadequate resources or time, personal problems and so on.

Once the reason is established, a confidential counselling session will have to produce clear guidelines for improvement in the future, with specific tasks, targets and time schedules. The manager's point of view has to be clearly stated to the employee, as well as the performance criteria. The next stage would involve careful monitoring of the particular person and give specific feedback on his/her efforts and actions.

7.   How would you dismiss an employee who is not performing adequately?

A: If, after two or more counselling sessions and simultaneous continuous performance monitoring, an employee fails to improve, dismissing him is probably the only option. It is in the best interest of the company to deal with non-productive people this way.

In the termination discussion, all necessary points have to be clarified and discussed, such as factual evidence of inadequate results, contributing factors, key reasons for the dismissal and detailed conditions of the dismissal or transfer. In some cases, when the employee has a history of accomplishments and could make a contribution to the company in a different position, a transfer is a viable option.

All applicable company rules and procedures would have to be followed, as well as any laws and regulations that govern this particular situation. All actions and conclusions would have to be well documented and the dismissed employee informed of all benefits and aids available (dismissal payment, personnel office help, job agencies, and so on).

Professional knowledge

An expert is one who knows more and more about less and less.

Nicholas Murray Butler

It is very difficult, almost impossible, to list, let alone answer, the specific questions of a technical or highly specialised nature, that interviewers may ask you. The questions will depend entirely on your occupation, the interviewer's knowledge of that area and the type of job you are being interviewed for.

The primary purpose of this section is to give you the idea of the format and content of specialised questions. Even the questions given here are still broad in content. Be prepared for very specific ones, such as: 'On the automation project mentioned, what brand of programmable logic controllers did you use and what software and graphic package did you install?'.

1. **Have you had any experience in ____?**

- *family law* (Lawyer)
- *high voltage switching* (Electrical Engineer)
- *AutoCad or computer drafting* (Draftsman)

2. **Your résumé states that you organised plant shutdowns and major periodical maintenance? How did you approach the whole process and what planning and monitoring methods did you use?** (Maintenance Planner)

3.   Give me an example of an industrial dispute that you handled recently.
     (Industrial Relations Officer)

4.   One of your achievements at ACME Company was the introduction of the MBO (Management by Objectives) technique. Could you briefly explain the reasons for that decision, the difficulties that you faced and name some benefits that resulted from it.
     (Department Manager)

5.   Tell me about an instance when you had to dismiss an employee who was not performing adequately.
     (Personnel Officer)

6.   How do you prepare yourself for a particularly difficult and important sales presentation?
     (Salesman)

7.   Every now and then we have a difficult task of establishing rapport with a particular child or the whole class. Tell me about some of your experiences. What methods do you normally use to solve this type of problem?
     (Teacher)

8.   Have you ever worked with UNIX operating system and what programming languages did you use?
     (Computer Programmer)

9.   Have you ever treated patients suffering from Parkinson's disease?
     (Medical practitioner)

Self-development

The only things worth learning are the things you learn after you know it all.

Harry S. Truman

1. **How do you keep informed about the developments and news in other departments/sectors of your company?**

A: I regularly attend departmental meetings and read the Company's newsletter, which helps me to stay attuned to current trends and developments. However, I gather most valuable information from my dealings with my colleagues in other sections and departments. Quite often we work together on different multi-disciplinary projects. That kind of interaction is very important, since it helps to promote understanding and appreciation of other people's jobs, and encourages teamwork.

2. **Do you subscribe to any trade/professional magazines? Which ones?**

A: I receive quite a few professional journals and some of them are particularly useful. I have been receiving _____ (*Machine Design, Computing, The International Medical Gazette, . . .*) for almost four years now.

3. **What are your current/future plans for self-improvement?**

A: My general goal is to keep learning, expanding my knowledge and improving my skills. Technology has been changing so rapidly that in order to keep pace with change one has to make constant self-improvement a top priority. Some of my education will be informal, through reading and learning in the job. I plan to take courses in _____ (*public speaking, word processing, child care*) at _____ (*college, university*).

4. **What are some of the areas in which you would like to improve in future?**

Mention an area not directly related to your work, something 'nice to have' rather than 'an absolute necessity' for the job.

A: Although my performance appraisals have been extremely positive, I would like to improve my _____ (*bookkeeping, computer, management*) skills. I find that area very important for my professional growth and my contribution to the employer.

5. **What have you accomplished in the line of self-improvement during the last year or two?**

A: Six months ago I ＿＿＿ (*obtained my bachelor's degree, started my studies towards a Master's degree*). I also attended a few ＿＿＿ (*recognised, university accredited, informal*) courses/workshops/ seminars. They helped me to improve my ＿＿＿ (*management skills, typing skills*).

I also received extensive training in my job that helped me to get promoted to ＿＿＿ (*shift supervisor, electrical inspector, senior analyst*).

6. Have you attended/participated in any professional seminars/conferences in the past year or two?

A: I recently published a paper and presented it at ＿＿＿ (*The Mining & Minerals Processing Conference, Electrical Energy Usage Symposium*). I also attended ＿＿＿ (*The Third International Conference on Vibration Monitoring, Real Estate Sales Seminar, National Accountancy Week*).

7. Were they company sponsored or did you do it at your own initiative and expense?

A: Some of the courses, mostly internal ones, were sponsored by the Company. I attended most of the external courses and conferences at my own expense. I regard that training as a valuable investment and an effective way to improve my skills and performance at work.

8. How do you see your present position changing over the next couple of years? What are you doing to prepare yourself for the changes ahead?

The answer to the first question will depend on your particular situation. In the second part of your answer, outline your plans for self-development and improvement or broadening of your skills.

Decision making

Decisiveness

1. **What kinds of decisions do you tend to make quickly and for which kind do you need more time?**
    In your answer, emphasise the fact that you generally make decisions quickly and stick to them, changing them slowly (only if necessary). These are the traits of successful people. You can utilise answers for questions 2 and 3 to expand on this.

2. **Tell me about the most difficult decisions you have made recently? Why were they difficult?**

    A: The most difficult decisions I made were those that either directly affected other people or had a big impact on my employer's success and profitability. One of the toughest was the decision to use a contract workforce for large projects and major maintenance work. I made that decision with higher efficiency, reliability and profitability in mind. On the other side were restricted work practices, high wages, overtime penalties and low morale and effectiveness of the permanent work force. That strategy meant a number of redundancies through retirements and lay-offs, but the bottom line is always the business itself. It has to survive, or a much higher number of people would be affected. Tough times do call for some tough measures.

3. **Have you ever delayed a decision to give yourself more time to think? What was the outcome of that decision?**

    A: There is always some vital information or fact that has to be known in order to make a right decision. If that information is not available and if delaying the decision would not have an impact on the result, I usually postpone making a decision until those critical pieces are put in place. That is my main reason for the occasional delay in making a decision.

    Very rarely do I need time to think about the problem. I make decisions fairly quickly and change them slowly, only if I see that the anticipated results may not be achieved that way.

Judgement

1.   **What are some of the most important decisions you have made in your life?**
     In your answer use examples such as a decision to migrate to another country, to change careers or move from town to town, to acquire a second degree, a post-graduate qualification, to join the Army, or anything as significant as that.

2.   **In your job, what decisions take you the longest time to reach?**
     Similar to question 1 under 'Decisiveness'.

3.   **Can you give me some examples of good and not so good decisions you have made recently?**
     When you mention some of the bad decisions you have made (as few as possible), quickly point out what corrective action you took and tell them about the eventual successful outcome.
A: I always feel it's better to take a calculated risk, to stand up and make a decision, even if it's the wrong one, than not to make a decision at all. Problems can not be solved by not taking action and by not making decisions.

4.   **What do you do when you have an important decision to make?**
A: Before making an important decision, I take three basic steps. First, I analyse all aspects of the issue and all possible consequences. Second, I try to anticipate potential problems that can affect the decision or be caused by it. Third, I talk to people who would be affected by that decision and get their input. By following these rules I make sure that the optimal option is chosen and that the right decision is made.

Problem solving

1.   **Have you ever recognised or noticed a particular problem before your colleagues or superiors?**

Emphasise the fact that you always keep your eyes and ears open. You continuously analyse trends and have the ability to notice problems at a very early stage. Employers like this kind of attitude.

A: On some occasions I noticed certain problems with a potentially serious impact on _____ (*production, safety, morale, efficiency*). Familiarisation with equipment and procedures is an important part of my job. It enables me to recognise and identify trends, patterns, potential problems and critical success factors at an early stage, usually earlier than others could notice them. (*Now add an example from your experience.*)

2. **How do you prepare yourself for potential problems?**

A: I always try to look at a problem as if for the first time. I don't bind myself to the ways the same or a similar problem was handled in the past. I don't assume anything and take nothing for granted. The only thing I know from the beginning is that the solution is there, it just has to be found.

3. **What problems that you are currently trying to solve came as a surprise to you? Was it possible to anticipate the occurrence of those problems?**

A: This is where know-how comes in. It isn't just expert knowledge mixed with the right kind of experience. It is the whole working philosophy that includes work ethics, motivation and efforts coupled with applicable experience and a professional way of thinking and problem solving.

The ability to anticipate problems and prepare for them in advance is of paramount importance in my occupation. However, some obstacles are very difficult, if not impossible, to predict or anticipate. One of our current problems is _____. It is a unique problem that hasn't happened before, and I have to come up with strategies that will help us solve it.

Risk taking

Risk varies inversely with knowledge.

Irving Fisher, *The Theory of Interest*

The first two questions under this heading require specific answers from an applicant, so instead of giving you complete model answers, I thought it more appropriate to point out a few important points to you. Use examples that will reinforce your image as a person prepared to take calculated risks when necessary, but also someone who is able to postpone a decision in certain circumstances in order to gather more information that is needed to make the right decision.

1. **What was the most risky decision you ever made? What was the outcome of that decision?**

2. **Describe a recent decision you made that involved more than the usual amount of risk.**

3. **Were there any decisions you made without having all necessary information? Why did you make those decisions without waiting for complete information?**

A: On one occasion I did make a decision without having complete information on the possible solutions. What I did know, however, was the problem, its symptoms and origins and its potential impact on the production and equipment. When I made the decision, prompt and energetic action was needed in order to prevent a major breakdown. Although taking a calculated risk can sometimes be justified, playing it safe is usually a much better approach.

4. **Describe a situation when you received a new procedure or instruction with which you disagreed. What action did you take and why?**

A: Although that shouldn't be the case, procedures and instructions are sometimes written by technical writers or administrative staff, not by experts. Whenever I faced such situations in the past, I made sure I talked to the originator of a particular material and to my superiors, explained why I disagreed and suggested corrections or measures for improving the inadequacies. (*Now add an example from your own experience.*)

5. **Tell me about a time when, after considering all pros and cons, you decided not to take any action, although you were under pressure to do so.**

The best reason you could use for postponing action would be waiting for the complete, or at least essential, information in order to prevent impulsive or irresponsible decision making. That will help you to project an image of a systematical, organised and cool-headed achiever, instead of a whimsical guesser.

6. **Do you think large companies, like your present employer, discourage employees from taking risks?**
   There are two possible paths here. If the company you are being interviewed by is one of the 'heavyweights', your answer is obvious. You like **big.** **Big** *is beautiful and* **big** *can and does encourage people to experiment and take risks.*

   If you are interviewing for a position with a smaller company, use this as one of your reasons for leaving or looking for another job with a smaller and more dynamic company, which encourages people to take risks. You like taking calculated risks and can display a successful history of good decisions and thrive on challenge.

7. **Are there any areas in your current job in which you feel you should have decision-making authority but do not?**
   This question gives you a chance to explore once more your capabilities and resources that haven't been fully utilised, or officially recognised, by your employer. Be careful not to sound bitter or disappointed and try not to display resentment or frustration towards your current employer (which is very easy, because it's probably one of the main reasons you are looking for another job)!

Safety

In today's employment climate, clouded with potential threats to employers, such as law suits, damage claims, worker's compensation payments and hefty penalties from various government departments, safety comes first and foremost. Reflect on that in your answers.

1. **Occasionally we have to bend the rules to get a particular job done. Have you ever done that and what was the outcome of your decision?**

A: I always observe safety rules and only in exceptional situations allow myself or my co-workers to 'bend' them a bit to get the job done. A few months ago _____. (*Give an example which involves a safe alternative to standard procedure and stress a satisfactory outcome which saved both time and money.*)

2. Describe a situation from your past experience when you noticed a task that was being done unsafely or a process that created a safety hazard. What did you do?

A: Quite a few times I have noticed tasks being performed in an unsafe or inefficient manner. On one occasion _____. (*Give an example.*) I wasn't involved in that project, but I warned the workers immediately and corrective action was taken. I also informed their supervisor. At the next safety meeting a new procedure was agreed upon and we haven't had any similar incidents since.

3. Have you ever had to reprimand or discipline an employee for not observing, or for violating, safety rules?

A: In the past I had to deal with frequent breaches of safety rules and company policies. Most incidents were of a repetitive nature _____ (*people not wearing safety glasses or hearing protection, not using the right tools, improper handling or weight lifting, etc.*).

I recognised it as a potential problem and enforced firm rules and reprimands for breaching them. The number of incidents of that kind has dropped significantly since then, and every employee now recognises the importance of safety rules.

4. Have you ever noticed a health or safety hazard before your colleagues or superiors? What was the problem and what course of action did you take?

A: On a few occasions I was the first to recognise a safety hazard. My experience in _____ (*fire fighting, waste management, maintenance methods*) helps me to discover potential hazards and take action to rectify problems and remove those dangers from the workplace. Whenever I notice something irregular or unsafe, I do the initial investigation and inform the internal safety committee.

5. **Were you ever injured in your job? What happened and what was the outcome of the accident?**

    Compete honesty is needed here. This type of information can be checked from various files and records, and if you suffered any permanent damage, the fact will be revealed during a medical examination.

A: No, I was never injured in my job. Observing safety rules is one of my first priorities, and everything I do, I do in a safe and efficient manner.

    or

    I suffered an _____ (*eye, elbow, spine, muscle*) injury _____ (*ten, five, two*) years ago. Although I wore the personal safety equipment at the time and observed all safety rules, owing to _____ (*the failure of machinery, equipment breakdown, low safety standards, . . .*) the injury occurred. I eventually recovered fully and no disability of any kind resulted.

Awareness (Internal/External)

1. **Tell me about some departments you interface with in your present position.**

    Explain the relationship and mutual dependency between your department and other departments and the frequency and methods used in communicating with them.

2. **What do you do when unable to solve a problem within your department?**

A: To achieve results in the shortest possible time we have to work closely with other departments. When I face a problem on which we need outside help, I explore all possibilities and consult my peers from other departments. Sometimes they suggest specific action and help us perform the actual tasks, or provide the complete solution for us. Which way is better or more efficient depends on each particular problem and in-house expertise.

3. **What organisational resources or services do you use most often?**

Depending on your job, you may be using drafting, secretarial, engineering, security services, or any other resources. Contract work forces and temporary employees could also be mentioned.

4. **How do you keep informed about new developments in other departments?**

A: The best way to keep informed about new developments is through regular contact with my colleagues in those departments, either personally or over the phone, and through departmental meetings which are held once a week. I am also kept informed through internal memos and notes.

5. **What methods do you use to find out what your competitors are doing?**

A: There are various methods that I use. Professional, trade and business magazines and other publications are a vital source of general information. I also cultivate business contacts through my colleagues in those companies. 'Inside' information is very valuable. Trade shows and exhibitions are a great place to meet people and talk to them, and they provide an excellent opportunity to evaluate products and services. Last, but not least, through regular contact with our suppliers and vendors, I usually find out some relevant information on other companies and their plans.

6. **What government bodies affect your company's operations and how?**

The answer to this question has to be tailored to suit your situation and the business you are in. Since you don't know the interviewer's attitude towards government departments, don't criticise, condemn or complain! Explain the difficulties you face and the steps you take to resolve them. The same applies for the next two questions.

7. **What future trends do you see in this industry?**

Make sure you include positive and optimistic statements regarding the company that is interviewing you, even if the future is gloomy. Don't be too pessimistic. Project enthusiasm and a strong belief in the future.

8. **What events outside your company affected your operations in the last year to two? How did you adapt to those
changes?**
*This is where your general knowledge of the industry you're in is
valuable. Some of the factors/events/developments you could mention: new government policies and regulations, changes in the
market, your competitors' actions, recession, deregulation of the
market, etc. The main point is to appear aware of the latest developments and project a flexible attitude by giving them examples of your
positive response to those changes!*

Career goals

*My interest is in the future because I am going to spend
the rest of my life there.*

Charles F. Kettering

1. **What are your career goals for the next five years? How do
you plan to achieve them?**
A: My career plan for the next few years is to improve my management and inter-personal skills further and assume higher responsibilities at _____ (*specify your goals*).

To achieve that major goal I'm planning to continue/start my post-
graduate studies in management and find a challenging position with
room for personal and professional growth and opportunities for
achieving tangible results and professional advancement. This
position suits my abilities well and opens new opportunities for
achieving success, which is my ultimate goal.

2. **Where do you see yourself in ten years' time?**
*Some interviewers will ask you a question about your long-term goals
and plans for achieving them. It's a difficult question to answer, but
try to prepare yourself. Don't answer something smart and ambitious
like 'Sitting in your chair'. Nobody likes jokes at their expense.*
A: In the next ten years I expect to progress through _____ (*junior
staff, management*) ranks to _____ (*management, supervisory,*

senior management) levels. By that time I will have further improved my technical skills and acquired business management skills.

3. **What steps have you already taken in order to achieve your goals?**
A: One of the most significant steps I've taken was applying for this job. The position could be significant for my future development, together with the additional qualifications I'm planning to obtain within _____ years. I have already started my further education in the area of _____ (*computer science, management techniques*).

4. **How does your current job relate to your career goals?**
   For people staying in the same career:
A: My present/former position fits/fitted well in my career plans. I learned a lot in that job, improved myself and my performance, achieved positive results and advanced through the levels. However, the current opportunities are somewhat limited at _____ (*your place of employment*), so I think that the time has come to move on. I'm ready for new challenges and increased responsibilities.
   For people changing careers:
A: After _____ (*number of years*) in _____ (*your present or former occupation*) I've decided to move into _____ (*your new profession*). This career turnaround hasn't come suddenly, I have always liked this profession and gradually mastered the skills needed to perform its tasks. I am ready to assume responsibility and start achieving results.

5. **Why do you think this job would help you achieve your career goals?**
   Important question. Prepare your answer carefully so you can show them that you understand the job you've been interviewed for and convince them that it matches your career plans.
A: I see this job as an opportunity to learn more about_____ (*marketing, desktop publishing, management*) and to utilise my skills to the fullest. This experience should assist me with my plans to become a _____ (*solicitor, chief engineer, senior lecturer*) within the next three years.

6.   What were your career goals when you graduated/left school? Do you think you have achieved them?

A: After graduation, my main career goal was to learn as much as possible in my chosen field. My first job with _____ was in line with that plan and helped me develop my potential. Another significant goal was to keep learning and improving my skills, not only in the job, but also through formal training and education towards a higher degree. I like my chosen field and I'm satisfied with the progression of my career so far, so I think I have achieved my original goals.

7.   Have you considered any alternative career path for the future?

A: I am very happy with my chosen profession and the progression of my career so far, so I haven't contemplated changing careers. However, should the right opportunity arise, I would consider such a move. I regard myself as very flexible and I leave my options open all the time.

8.   Should you be offered this job, when would you expect a promotion?

A: I believe promotions should not be expected, they should be earned. After mastering this position, realising successful completion of my tasks and making a significant contribution to this company, I would be ready for new achievements, should the opportunity arise.

9.   How long would you stay with the company should you get this job?

A: This position fits well into my career plans and I can see a lot of potential for growth in your company. I expect to start being productive very early, and as long as I keep developing my skills, contributing to the company's success and growing in the job, there would be no reasons for me to leave.

10.   How important to you is the opportunity to advance your career and, eventually, to reach the top?

A: Reaching the top is a very relative term. Doing a good and professional job for my employer is the most important issue to me.

Once you concentrate on good performance and on constant improvement of your knowledge and skills, the advancement will come naturally. If by reaching the top you mean being a top performer and being successful in my occupation, I do consider reaching the top as very important.

11.   Would you consider switching careers in the future, should the opportunity arise?
The answer to this question should be identical or similar to the answer of question 7.

12.   How long have you been looking for a job?
Even if you have been seeking alternative employment for some time, do not admit it. Tell them that you've just started to look for another job. The story is different if you are unemployed. In that case the interviewer probably won't ask you this question. The answer would be obvious from your résumé.
A: This is my first interview for some time. Although I have been monitoring the job market closely, I've decided to seek alternative employment very recently. The downturn in the industry, lack of opportunities at my present position and my readiness for new achievements prompted me to look for other opportunities.

13.   Have you had interviews with other companies recently? How did you do?
This is a typical knockout question. Beware. Never admit that you were unsuccessful at other interviews. The interviewer's logic is: 'If he wasn't good enough for them, he can't be good for us, either'.
A: I haven't had any recent interviews, but in the past, a very high percentage of my interviews resulted in job offers. The employers recognised my talents and experience and offered me positions of increased responsibility.

14.   What references do you think your current employer would give you?
A: All my references have always been very good, so I am sure that my present employer would give me an excellent reference.

15. **Does your present employer know that you have been looking for another job?**

A: I haven't told my present employer that I've been exploring other employment possibilities. Once I'm offered a job, I will let them know about my plans and intentions.

or

Yes, my employers know that I have been exploring other employment opportunities, but should you wish to talk to them, please let me know in advance, so I can talk to them first.

Work experience and employment history

The way to avoid mistakes is to gain experience. The way to gain experience is to make mistakes.

Job hunters' Catch-22

1. **How did you get your first job after graduation? How difficult was it to get into _____ (the oil and gas industry, mining, the hospitality industry, corporate finance)?**

A: During my summer holidays I worked for a few well-known companies in my field. I gained valuable experience there and established important business contacts. After graduation one of those companies had a vacant position for a graduate _____ (*surveyor, chemist, engineer*). The position called for someone with strong inter-personal and analytical skills and a good honours degree. I was selected from the pool of applicants and given a chance to learn and prove myself in that demanding but interesting job.

2. **How do you think you benefited from your first job? What do you consider your most valuable experience gained in that job?**

A: The transition from university to industry was a crucial step in my career. Education prepared me well for the intellectual challenges that lay ahead, but most practical skills I possess I have learned in the job. I have learned how to apply my knowledge to a variety of problems, how to make decisions and set goals and priorities. I have become familiar with standards, legal requirements of the professional and various policies and procedures. I would consider the ability to relate to people and work as part of a team, and to achieve tangible results, the most valuable experience gained in that job.

3. **Why did you leave your job at ____ Company? Did you consider that move to be a promotion or a lateral move?**

A: Although I learned a lot in that job, I felt that while I was specialising in certain areas of ____, I lacked experience in other aspects of the job, namely ____ *(banking, insurance, design)*. My subsequent position offered new challenges and opportunities for growth. I gained a much broader range of skills and was given more responsibility. I consider that move, which was by no means a lateral one, the best decision in my career.

4. **Have you ever changed jobs or companies purely for monetary gain?**

Your answer should be no. You have to project an image of a person who values the company, the job and co-workers more than monetary rewards.

A: Although I consider remuneration an important motivational factor, it is of secondary importance. The job itself, its tasks, the work environment and the opportunity to learn and participate in new and exciting developments, and become an efficient member of a team, are to me the most significant aspects of a job. When I changed jobs, it was never for monetary gain only.

5. **Have you ever been promoted within the same company? How did you feel about that move? Was it in line with your career objectives?**

If you have been promoted, mention your strengths, qualities and achievements that were the reason for promotion. Emphasise that you welcomed the promotion and were further motivated by additional authority and responsibilities.

6. **Why were you made redundant from your job with ____?**

If your job was made redundant, it's the company's failure, not yours. Despite giving your best, your employer didn't know how to utilise your talents and abilities. It's a sad old story where people get blamed for the failure of the system. Employers will never admit that their systems are wrong, it's much easier to blame individuals.

A: At the time the company was going through a long period of heavy losses, owing to bad management and the impact of the recession on the industry. Some radical actions were taken by senior management, and the whole supervisory and some professional levels were made redundant. Sadly, the criteria were not performance and individual efforts, but rather the length of service and the nature of the position. Since I was one of the newer employees, my position was terminated.

7.   **What areas or aspects of your present/previous job do/did you like most?**
When answering this question, make sure you address some aspects of the job you have applied for, in order to create an impression that you would like the same things in your new job, should you get it.

A: I certainly like some aspects of my present job. It's a dynamic, hard-driving job that requires good decision-making and communication skills. I like constant interaction with people and the benefits of working in a team with other professionals. The job enabled me to strengthen my _____ (*practical, theoretical, management*) skills and prepared me well for my future career.

8.   **Are there any tasks or areas in your present position that have changed since you started in that job?**
There is no such thing as a static job. Every job changes from time to time and your aim here is to emphasise the positive changes that took place, especially if it was you who initiated them and/or carried them out.

A: From the day I started in my present position I kept learning and growing. I put a lot of time and effort into my career. As I mastered the job, my tasks become more and more complex and demanding. I became involved in various additional activities and the whole scope of the position changed. I was given more authority and made responsible for _____. That way I was able to broaden my experience and update my skills and knowledge related to those activities.

9. **I see from your résumé that you owned a small business a couple of years ago. How much benefit did you get out of that experience?**

Designed for people who owned a small business, but, owing to various problems, went back to the security of permanent employment, this question could invoke bitterness and resignation. Don't let it happen. Emphasise positive aspects and all the useful things that you learned as a business owner, from accounting skills to orientation towards customer satisfaction.

A: The experience I gained while running a small business has proved extremely valuable in my career. I acquired a good working knowledge in various disciplines such as accounting, taxation, profit and loss control, logistics, negotiation and planning. I learned even more about people, how to treat customers and vendors, how to get cooperation from them and how to keep them happy and satisfied with my products and services.

10. **Tell me about some of the knowledge and experience you have gained in your present position that you could use in this job?**

Always keep in mind that employers try to predict your future behaviour and achievements on the basis of your past. They reason that everything you've done in the past will be, or at least, could be, repeated in future. That applies to both your strong points and achievements and to your shortcomings and mistakes. This question confirms that line of thinking. To answer it, you have to know the job you've applied for really well, and use that knowledge when emphasising your capability to perform the main tasks of the position.

11. **What were the reasons for the gaps in your employment history?**

This answer will again depend on your particular situation. The interviewer wants you to tell him the reasons that caused those gaps, such as maternity leave, serious or prolonged illness or disability, inability to find any work, periods spent at home taking care of your family, etc. Whatever your reasons are, always emphasise the fact that you are able to re-enter the workforce and achieve results in new jobs. Your explanation of the facts should be concise and to the point.

Don't go around the bush, avoid answering or blame others. Flawless careers are rare: we are all human and we all make mistakes.

12. **You have changed jobs quite a few times within the last few years. What were the reasons for that?**
    Even if it's true, don't say something like 'I usually get bored doing the same job after a couple of years, so I looked for a change' or 'I had some debts, so I used every opportunity to get a better-paying job'.

A: I've changed jobs according to my career plans. The main reason was to gain experience in various aspects of _____ (*management, medicine, human resource management*) and broaden my horizons. I was able to recognise opportunities and to capitalise on them.

13. **Would you recommend your present employer to others?**
    Another knockout question. Say only good things about your former or current employer. Your message should be: 'It's a great place to work' (but not for you).

A: I can say only good things about my present employer. I was treated with respect and given every opportunity to participate in various activities and achieve both the employer's and my professional goals.

   Owing to the _____ (*downturn in the industry, lack of funds or new contracts, company's restructuring plans, limited opportunities for advancement*) I have decided to explore other employment opportunities. However, for someone with less experience who is interested in that type of work, it would be a great place to work.

14. **What do you consider your biggest achievement or the most important idea you have implemented in your career?**
    The answer has to be tailored to suit your work experience. Although the question asks for a single, most important contribution, you can mention more than one, especially if they could be relevant to the company that's interviewing you.

15. **I've heard stories about the bad feelings between your present employer and unions and how the company treats its employers badly. Are they true?**

Another knockout question. Never discuss rumours about your employers, or, heaven forbid, internal secrets and confidential information. You have to project an image of a trustworthy employee who can keep secrets and be loyal to his employer. If you bad-mouth your present employer, the interviewer can expect the same to happen to him, further down the track. him, further down the track.

A: I'm really not sure. I haven't heard any of those rumours myself. My priority is to concentrate on my performance and represent the company to the best of my abilities. To me, there is no room for rumours in a productive environment, where lines of communication are open.

Suitability for the job

1. **Why would you like to work for this company?**
   This is probably the most important question in every job interview. You can be sure that it will be on every interviewer's list, therefore you should prepare yourself for it. Spend as much time as you need rehearsing your answer; your efforts will be rewarded. The next question is similar and should be treated with equal caution.

2. **Why did you apply for this particular position?**
   A: First and foremost, I'm well qualified for this job and able to make a significant contribution to your company. This position suits my skills, talents and career plans, and has a lot of advancement opportunities to offer. Last, but not least, the outstanding reputation of your company was a significant factor that influenced my decision to apply.

3. **How will our company benefit from hiring you?**
   This question is a natural follow-up from the previous ones. Even if they don't ask you directly, it is always on their mind, and whatever you say at a job interview should address it in one way or the other. A very important opportunity to summarise all your strong points, skills and abilities and to talk in terms of benefits. Put yourself in the employer's shoes and tell them everything you can do for them.

4. **What do you know about our company?**
    This is a good opportunity to display your knowledge and show them that you've done some thorough research on the company. Start with the company's mission statement, main locations, products, key people. Cover the current plans and actions, such as expansions, investments, and finish with future plans, long range goals and your view of the company's future (it has to be a pink one). Always project enthusiasm and sincere interest. Don't criticise, condemn or complain.

5. **Do you have any friends or relatives working for this company?**
    If you do, say so. That fact can be checked, so the truth is best here. In some cases, having a relative who is a hard worker and a reputable person may help you, too, to be perceived as such.

A: A good friend of mine works in your Manchester office. I don't know anybody here in Birmingham.

6. **How did you find out about this vacancy?**
    If the vacancy was advertised, you probably won't be asked this question. If it wasn't, tell them the truth: a friend told you about it, you offered your services without knowing that there was a vacancy, or whatever the case is.

A: I have been interested in your company for some time, so I was familiar with your plans for expansion and growth and anticipated a vacancy of this kind. I then decided to offer my services to you.

7. **How confident are you in your ability to handle this position?**

A: I am very confident in my abilities. I learn quickly and it shouldn't take me long to achieve results in this job. Starting a new job is always difficult, but I make an extra effort to become productive in the shortest time possible. I already know most of the job requirements, so once I familiarise myself with the place and establish the right relationships with other members of your team, all ingredients for success will be there.

8. **What particular strengths and qualifications would you bring to this job?**

Similar to the previous question, just shift the emphasis from their benefits to your capabilities and strengths.

9. Do you think your lack of experience would affect your performance in this job?

You'll have to compensate for lack of experience. Use experience gained in similar areas, portable skills (those you can apply in the new job), and your knowledge, as substitutes for relevant experience.

A: I may not have had many years of experience in this field, but my knowledge and ability to learn quickly and work hard will enable me to make immediate contributions to this job. With some specialised training and my desire to learn and improve myself, I could accomplish a lot in this position,

10. Don't you think you are over-qualified for this position?

They fear that you will leave as soon as a better opportunity comes up. You have to reassure them using the following ideas: there are always new things to be learned in any job, you are particularly interested in that job and you would stay as long as you keep contributing to the employer's success.

This question can also be a hint that you are too old for a job or that they can't pay you as much money as you were earning before.

A: In every position there are always new skills to be mastered and new knowledge to be acquired. However, my experience in similar positions will enable me to do the required tasks fast, with confidence and with minimum training and supervision. Therefore, as the company would not have to train me in all aspects of the job, there would be an immediate return on your investment in me and my services. This company provides a lot of opportunities for people with talent and the right qualifications, and could certainly benefit from my knowledge.

11. Would you agree to a three-month probationary period?

Three or six months' probation is mandatory with some employers (especially government departments), it's got nothing to do with your abilities. If that isn't the case, the interviewer is not totally convinced that you are the ideal person for the job, so you have to reassure him.

A: I can see no problems with a probationary period. I am a fast learner and it shouldn't take me long to prove myself and assume all responsibilities of the position.

12.   **Are you prepared to accept a position as a trainee?**
If you are, say so. If not, tell them why. Some employers cannot comprehend that a person of talent and experience would be insulted to start at the bottom. Once you start low, it's going to take longer to reach the top. Some employers will try to get you cheap by offering you to start at the entry level. The usual justification is lack of relevant experience. Don't fall for this trick.

A: Yes, I am. I haven't had much experience in this area and I would welcome the opportunity to learn and get a good foundation in this business. I can use a good deal of my knowledge and experience, so it shouldn't take me long to master this job and assume bigger responsibilities.
or
I have had a number of years of related experience, so all I need to learn are some specific details and methods this company uses, which should not take long. I am capable of doing all tasks of this position efficiently and without supervision. I'm a self-starter and can bring maturity and responsibility to this position. You could utilise my strengths and talents much better in a higher and more demanding position.

13.   **Do you think you possess a skill or knowledge that could give you an edge over other candidates?**
A ridiculous question, but, sadly, a very common one. How would you know who your competitors are? The best strategy is to tell them you are not familiar with your competitors' skills and knowledge, and then repeat what your strengths are and what you could do for the employer, if selected.

14.   **Are you looking for a permanent or temporary assignment?**
By the time you are interviewed, it should be clear both to you and to the interviewer what type of position you have applied for, so this question will not be asked too often. Should you approach an employer directly, without an advertised vacancy, you can expect this question.

A: I am looking for a permanent position, but should you have a temporary opening only, I may be prepared to accept it if it fits into my career plans.

15. **This job requires frequent motorway travel. Would that create a problem for you?**

Count your blessings. You may disagree, but this is your opportunity to travel free, see places and meet people.

A: I have always enjoyed travel. That was one of the reasons for choosing this type of work. I have travelled extensively in the past, owing to the nature of my previous positions, and I would welcome the opportunity to establish contacts and work in different parts of the country.

16. **Do you have any questions about the company or the vacancy?**

This is usually the interviewer's last, closing question. The ball is now in your court, so make sure you kick it hard. This is probably your only opportunity to find out any fine details about the job and the people you'll be working with, should you get it.

Some typical questions are listed on pages 183–185, but you can ask anything you like. Just make sure that by asking each particular question you gain points. If you are not sure about any question, if there is a danger that the question may make you look dumb, misinformed, naïve, boasting, selfish or insensitive, don't ask it.

17. **Tell me about some of the first things you would do in this job?**

A: My first task would be to establish a productive and professional relationship with my co-workers. Learning about the company's policies and procedures is another very important step in the familiarisation process, as is becoming familiar with all aspects of the position and all job requirements. These initial tasks would make me ready to meet all demands and produce results in a very short time.

18. **This is the organisation chart of our department. Do you think you could work within this structure?**

A: This organisational structure seems fine to me, and I'm sure I
      would fit in quite nicely. The management structure is pretty lean
      and probably very efficient. The overall scheme looks effective and
      well balanced.

**19.   There are quite a few smokers in our office. As a non-
        smoker, do you see that as a problem?**

A: As long as my work area is free from smoke I don't mind other people
      smoking in the building. It's their personal choice. If it started
      affecting my work and productivity, I would classify it as a concern.

**20.   Have you got any concerns about this position or the
        company?**

      *This is a good opportunity for any questions you want to ask. Don't
      enquire about money and benefits. Leave that issue to the interviewer
      to bring up. Concentrate on the position, previous people in it,
      advancement opportunities, training and learning. You can also ask
      about company's plans and goals. If you haven't got any questions:*

A: I had many questions I wanted to ask you, but during our conversa-
      tion you covered all of them very well. I have a detailed picture of
      the position and the company, and feel that this position suits my
      skills and talents extremely well.

21.   Do you own your tools and equipment needed for the job?

A: I have made an investment in the equipment needed to do my job
      properly and professionally.
      *(List some examples, and don't forget your professional library, if
      relevant.)*
      or
      The equipment and tools I needed were provided by my former
      employer. However, if this position requires it, I would be happy to
      buy my own tools and equipment.

22.   Should you be offered this position, when could you start?

A: I have to give my present employer two weeks' notice. If it suits
      you, I could start right after that period. I would prefer an early
      start myself, so I can meet my future colleagues and prove myself
      in the job as soon as possible.

——————— Outside interests ———————

What we do during our working hours determines what we have; what we do in our leisure hours determines what we are.

George Eastman, founder of Kodak

1. **What are your hobbies, interests and leisure time activities?**
   This question needs a balanced answer. A bit of this and a bit of that. If the interviewer looks like a sport orientated person, emphasise your outdoor lifestyle and sport achievements.

   Passive hobbies (reading, listening to music, chess) are viewed less favourably than active ones by most interviewers. For some 'intellectual' positions, such as educational appointments, research or scientific jobs, physically passive hobbies and interests, such as reading, astronomy, writing, and so on, may be regarded as desirable and project the right image of the applicant.

2. **Do you prefer watching sport events on television or actively participating in them?**
   Active participation in sports is viewed favourably. It tells them that you are a team player and that you know how to observe the rules and work towards a common goal. Watching sport events makes you a couch potato.

   A: Although I don't mind watching top sport events occasionally, I prefer active participation, especially in team sports. It helps me keep fit and feel good, and is also a great way of socialising.

3. **Do you prefer team sports or individual ones?**
   If the job you have applied for requires teamwork (most jobs do), tell them you prefer team sports. If it's a 'lone wolf job' (astronomer, writer), individuality is a plus.

   A: I don't differentiate between team and individual sports. Both kinds have their strong points; teamwork and team spirit on one hand and individual strength and self-reliance on the other. To me, the most important aspects of sport are achievements and hard work. I prefer active participation in sports. Apart from the obvious benefits, such as fitness and stamina, sport helps me develop my people-management skills, team spirit and ability to work with others towards a common goal.

4. **What is your favourite sport?**
The answer should be similar to the one in previous question. Don't mention any destructive sport, such as boxing or mud-wrestling, unless applying for a position where those skills could prove useful (a bouncer in a nightclub, policeman or bodyguard).

5. **What newspapers and magazines do you read regularly?**
The safest bet is to go for trade or professional magazines. Tell them you read 'Penthouse' and watch the interest fade.
A: I regularly read professional magazines such as *Architectural Review* and *Interior Design*, to which I subscribe. My wife subscribes to *International Business Week*, which I also find very informative.

6. **Do you subscribe to any of them?**
A: I subscribe to *Bulletin* and *Business Review Weekly*. They cover a wide range of business and management topics, as well as current trends and news.

7. **What sections in a newspaper or a magazine do you find most interesting?**
It would be a mistake to offer sport pages or comics as an answer (although I know many professional people who read only sport pages). The business section is always the safest bet, although anything that can help you project a systematic, business-orientated and creative image is welcome. Current affairs (local, national and international) is also a safe bet, but use it as a last resort.

8. **What are your favourite television programmes?**
This is a knockout question. Avoid brain washers like Roseanne or Emmerdale. Go for something scientific, Tomorrow's World, businesslike, The Money Programme or political, World in Action.

A: I don't have much time for television. It's not high on my list of priorities, but I enjoy some programmes, such as news, current affairs, business reviews and scientific programmes like *Tomorrow's World*.

9. **Does your social life include colleagues or co-workers?**
Tell them you don't differentiate between people. Your friends come from all spheres of life. Some of them are your old school friends, some are your colleagues or business acquaintances. That projects a balanced attitude towards life and relationships.

A: Some of my friends are also my co-workers. We share the same interests and a similar lifestyle and feel close to each other, probably because of our close and productive relationships at work. I have many other friends and acquaintances, old friends from school and university, neighbours and others.

10. **Do you prefer activities at home, with your family, or the outdoor lifestyle?**
A balanced approach is needed again. Since you work hard and long hours, you don't have much leisure time. For that reason you use every minute of it to be with your family, either indoors or outdoors.

A: I try to mix both, if possible. During summer, we tend to spend most of our time together outside the house, around the pool, in the country or playing sports. In winter, because of less favourable weather conditions, much more time is spent indoors or visiting friends.

11. **What types of books do you like? Can you name a few of your favourites?**
Don't mention this book or any other book on interviewing or job hunting. Don't even mention self-improvement books. Select something appropriate, not too shallow or scandalous, like Jackie Collins, not too intellectual, like Dostoevski or Umberto Eco. Moderation is needed here. Autobiographies of successful business people are not a bad choice.

12. **Do you drink alcohol at home or on social occasions?**
Never admit that you drink more than the usual amount. The

occasional glass of wine or a beer with friends is OK. And another point – never drink before the interview. Some people go for a nip of spirit, for courage. Don't. Use coffee or herbal teas for calming effect (if you are a nervous type). Never concede that you drink alone. It creates a bad image of antisocial behaviour; most alcoholics drink alone.

A: I don't mind the occasional drink with friends or business acquaintances, but drinking is not really my style.

— Salary history and requirements —

All questions in this section serve the same purpose. They help employers to establish your price, i.e. the lowest offer you would accept. The starting salary is extremely important, owing to the fact that employers think in percentage points. They say: 'Last year we gave you a ten per cent rise while the management got only five!', forgetting that ten per cent of say, £25,000 pa is much less than 5 per cent of £75,000! Once you start low, it's very difficult to get a decent rise (in absolute terms)!

Your salary history should be used only as an indication of your progress and achievements. The salary levels in the past should have nothing to do with your future salary. Each job is different and the remuneration packages have to be different. By telling the interviewers your present or previous salary, you automatically place an upper limit on their offers.

If you have to tell them the figure, think of all possible benefits you are or were getting and add 5 per cent to 10 per cent to it. Find out how much say, a company car, is worth to your present employer. It may be worth only £2000 per year to you, but it's probably worth close to £4000–£8000 to them. In short – boost it. Even if they try to check your salary, your former employers will not tell them. The secrecy of the pay system is finally working for you!

1. **Can you give me a short overview of your salary history?**
    Avoid numbers, if you can. Concentrate on other benefits such as job satisfaction, personal growth and improvement or increased achievements.

A: I would be glad to tell you exact figures and dates, but I am not able to recite them from memory, because of regular pay increases and *promotions. The money side of those jobs was not as important to me as the opportunity to learn and perform in the job. My employment record shows a continuous trend in salary growth.*

2.   Have you ever been refused a salary increase (pay rise)?

A: Due to my positive performance appraisals I haven't had to ask my superiors for a pay rise. The salary reviews resulted in consistent increases in line with my contributions. That means I was never refused a raise on the basis of inadequate performance.

3.   What is your present salary?

Make sure you take every penny into account. The higher you can quote without lying, the stronger your bargaining position will be. Start low and they'll offer you low.

A: With a fortnightly bonus, overtime, company contributions to my superannuation fund, extra holiday pay, and a company car, my package is around £30,000 per year.

4.   How much would you like to be earning in five or ten years' time?

A: Since I strive constantly to achieve above average results and contribute to my company's profitability, I expect the remuneration to reflect my efforts and to be competitive with what similar positions pay at that time.

5.   What salary do you think you are worth?

A: Our worth is measured by our contributions to the employers. My personal credo is to perform to the best of my abilities and to contribute as much as I can. Therefore, I expect to advance in accordance with my efforts and achieved results and I'm sure that the right employer will recognise a job well done and be fair in putting a price tag on my work.

6.   Do you think people in your occupation are paid enough?

Be careful. You are walking on thin ice. Some people are grossly underpaid. If you are one of them, keep it to yourself. Don't let your anger and frustration show! There is nothing you can gain by speaking up (it is very unlikely that they would change their salary structure just because of you), but there is a lot to lose.

A: I think that no matter how much people earn, they would always strive for an even higher figure. It seems that is a human nature. However, the answer to this question is a very complex one. There are quite a few factors to be considered, such as the status of a particular profession in society, education levels, supply and demand for that type of service, contribution to the community as a whole, and, above all, the competence and integrity of the person doing the job. The most important aspect is the contribution people make to their employers and the quality of their work. The rewards usually follow automatically.

7.   **Should you join this company, would you be interested in becoming a member of our pension plan?**
Your message should reflect your attitude: you are not thinking about retirement, only about contributing to the well-being of the company that is interviewing you.

A: After careful consideration of the plan's structure and competitiveness in the financial market, I would be happy to join should it prove to be performing and providing a good return on the invested funds.

8.   **Do you have any additional income?**
This is none of their business. If you want to be honest, go ahead, but you may risk being offered a lower salary. Remember the employers' tendency to pay a low salary and expect a miraculous performer on their payroll? This question is one of their tools for saving some money. I prefer the second option – no outside income.

A: I occasionally do some _____ (*baby-sitting, tutoring, etc.*) in the evenings and some part-time work at weekends as a _____ (*bartender, gardener, handyman*) but I have no regular commitments that could have an impact on my job. It is purely an extra source of income to help me achieve my financial goals.
or
I don't have any outside income (*much better answer*).

9.   **How much would you lower your expectations if the salary you are aiming for is higher than the salary package we are offering for this position?**
This smart question demands a smart answer. The core of it is: I am not prepared to lower my expectations. Wrap it up and you get this:

A: The salary itself is just one component of the whole offer. Should the working conditions, future prospects and opportunities for advancement be favourable, I would consider a figure slightly below my expectations. However, it would be difficult to accept less than my present salary. My salary history shows a consistent upward trend as a direct result of my performance and achievements, and I intend to continue that trend.

10. **To be honest, we'll have to decide between you and another candidate. We think either of you would be suitable for the job, so it comes down to money. What is the lowest salary you are prepared to accept?**
    Beware of this question. Whoever uses this tactic is a shrewd interviewer. He's intimidating you and playing you against other candidates. You can bet that he asked the other interviewee(s) the same question.

A: My work record shows increasing levels of responsibility and achievement and my salary history follows that trend. For a person with my qualifications and experience, and taking into account the complexity and importance of this position and the contributions that I could make in this job, a salary of _____ (*name the lowest figure you would accept, and as much as you think the interviewer would consider paying you*) is the absolute minimum.

— Your questions for the interviewer —

It is better to know some of the questions than to know all of the answers.

James Thurber

About the company/department

- What are the company's plans for the future?
- What new products is the company working on and planning to introduce?

- How does the company compare with its competitors?
- Is the company considering opening new plants or new ventures.
- Is the company considering any acquisitions?
- Are any cuts in the work force planned for the immediate future?
- How is the department organised?
- How is the department viewed by the management and other departments?
- What are the department's overall functions and responsibilities?

About the position

- How long has the position been vacant?
- How many employees have held the position in the last five/ten years?
- Why have they left?
- What are the most important duties of the position as perceived by the company?
- How much have the position, it's duties and scope changed in the last five/ten years?
- How does the position fit into the overall company structure?

About your direct supervisor (boss)

- Who does the position report to?
- Who does the supervisor report to?
- What is the supervisors's background?
- What is the supervisor's management style?

About salary and benefits

- Does the company have a formal salary structure with well-defined levels, or a more flexible one?
- What is the salary range for this position?

- How often are salaries reviewed?
- What factors determine the reviewed salary levels?
- Are there any incentive schemes in place?
- What insurance benefits are provided by the company?
- Is there a profit-sharing scheme?
- Are any relocation expenses met by the company?
- Is there a superannuation plan available? How much does the company contribute? How much do the employees contribute?
- Is there any annual extra holiday pay?

About advancement opportunities

- How many employees have been promoted from the position in the last five/ten years?
- What are the opportunities for advancement into management?
- Are there formal training programs available? How do they work?
- What factors are used to determine promotion eligibility?

—————— Illegal questions ——————

Twenty years ago, employers had few legal obligations in the hiring process. Today, things are very different. A whole myriad of laws, legislation and acts affect the process. Interviewers are very limited in terms of the questions they are allowed to ask. The following information should not be used in the hiring process and any question addressing these issues may be illegal:

- Race;
- Religion;
- National origin;
- Marital status;
- Sex (gender);
- Number of children;
- Affiliations with and membership of legal organisations;
- Handicaps.

Any question that deals with the issues above may be breaching one or more of the applicable laws and acts. Your task is to recognise those questions and form your answers in one of the few possible ways. Of course, not every question probing those areas is illegal, what can make it illegal is the way in which it is asked! Basically, anything that bears no significance to the particular job you have applied for, or to your capability to perform in that job, is irrelevant and probably illegal!

When asked an illegal question, you have four choices.

1. Answer it honestly.
The best option in some cases, but should the question be intimidating or too personal I would suggest one of the more advanced strategies. If they ask you awkward questions now, can you imagine what working for those people would be like later?

2. Answer it, but tell them what they want to hear.
This is the option I would recommend in most cases. If the interviewer asks you an illegal or tasteless question, you have a moral right not to tell the truth. Illegal questions are always transparent, i.e. it's very easy to see what the interviewer is getting at, therefore it is very easy to fabricate the answer he wants to hear.

3. Counterattack with a question, preferably a humorous one.
If asked 'What is your religion?' you can say 'Does your firm represent any particular sect?' Or for the question 'Which method of contraception do you use?', a good answer would be 'Which one do most of your employees prefer?'.

4. Politely refuse to answer.
In an ideal world this would be the ideal response. In the real world, it is not recommended. By refusing to answer you minimise your chances of getting the job. You may preserve your pride and dignity, but your stomach needs food, remember?

7

— CLOSING THE DEAL —

──────── **Salary-negotiating tactics** ────────

It is a well-known proposition that you know who's going to win a negotiation: it's he who pauses the longest.

Robert Holmes à Court, *Sydney Morning Herald*, 24 May 1986

Your objectives

In any negotiating process, be it negotiating when buying a house or talking about your future salary, there are two major objectives:

- to change the interviewer's impression of the strength of *your* position;
- to change the interviewer's impression of the strength of *his* position.

That's why you should project an image of a job-chooser, not a job-beggar. The interviewer can sense how you feel about yourself. Your task is to lure him into thinking that you have more than one ace up your sleeve. Once he starts thinking that way, your value can only go one way – up.

When the time comes for financial negotiation, what counts is not how much you are really worth, it's how much the interviewer thinks you're worth! Remember these words. At the job interview, which lasts on average around an hour, you cannot present your *complete self* to the interviewer. All you can create is a positive *image* of yourself, that will make employers eager to have you on their payrolls.

Salary negotiation is an elaborate game in which anything can be used as a tool. Bluffing is particularly useful. Employers use it quite often. Whenever they tell you something like: 'The salary for this position is £20,000', or 'We cannot go above £22,000', you know that they are prepared to go as high as £26,000 or even £28,000.

Money, benefits and substitutes

> *A negotiator should observe everything. You must be part Sherlock Holmes, part Sigmund Freud.*
>
> Victor Kiam, *Going For It*

Beware of the substitutes for money. They are usually called benefits. Your main task is to analyse them and to put a price tag on them, i.e. to establish how much each benefit is worth to you. Some benefits do have a certain value. They are:

- superannuation (pension plan benefits);
- company cars;
- private health insurance;
- air fares (for people living and/or working outside major centres);
- holiday pay;
- bonus schemes;
- company's share plans (discounted shares);
- subsidised housing;
- approved study leave;
- subsidised rents, telephone bills, rates, etc.

However, there are some substitutes used by employers to attract the naïve candidates. Most of the commonly used substitutes are basically useless from material point of view.

- **Fancy titles** are a form of psychological compensation. They usually hide dull jobs and make people feel better about doing jobs below their capabilities. How would you like telling your 'potential' girlfriend that you work as a garbage collector or a liftboy? Environmental technician and elevator supervisor sound much nicer.
- **Promises**. Not worth a penny. Once the employers get you on their payroll, they tend to forget what they promised. Always get promises in writing. Even then, what can you do if the employers don't fulfil them? Complain, threaten legal action and possibly risk being sacked? Not likely.
- **'The opportunity for growth'**. A very common promise in job advertisements. It still isn't clear to me what employers mean by that. Growth of your salary, professional growth, growth of your frustration, or what? In most cases it may mean growth of your responsibilities and an increase in overtime work, with no reward whatsoever.

What will your hourly rate be?

One of the shrewdest tactics used by employers is definitely a 'work now, we'll pay you later' philosophy. Any employee who doesn't get paid for overtime is a victim of this plot. Employees were told that *occasional* overtime would be required and that their salary packages were created with that in mind.

Take this example. Say you were offered a position as a mechanical engineer, with salary of £26,000 per annum, which is current market rate for an engineer with five to seven years' experience. For a standard 40 hour week your hourly rate would be £12.50. Sounds fine. In a few months time you realise that, due to the workload, you are putting in 55 hours a week. Your effective hourly rate is just over £9 per hour! By accepting these terms you reduced your salary to around £19,000 per annum, which is a starting salary for inexperienced graduates. So, what have you achieved? You've just gone back five to seven years!

Never think in 'per annum' terms. What matters
is your hourly rate. That's how much you're
worth.

Superannuation (Pension Plans)

Most employers offer their employees some sort of a pension plan. Some of them are contributory (employees contribute a certain percentage of their salaries), some aren't. In any case, all they offer is time: the longer you contribute to the fund, the better off you'll be at the end. The basic idea of creating a 'nest-egg' for your retirement is appealing, however, there is another point of view.

Superannuation funds usually reflect the employer's financial position. The better the company's performance, the stronger the fund. There is only one problem: if the company made a profit this year, why do you have to wait ten or twenty years to get your share? This is a typical 'work now, we'll pay you later' plot. Furthermore, they'll use your money for ten or twenty years, so, basically, you are lending out your money and, incidentally, being taxed twice in the process (once before they deduct your contributions from your salary, and once when you retire or resign and take the lump sum).

It seems that the whole scheme was designed to ensure the employer's hold over you and to take away your freedom of choice. Ambitious people, who want fast advancement, are the ones most affected. No matter when you leave the company, you can be sure that the benefits will be much less than the ones you would receive had you stayed there till retirement.

Avoid companies that use 'Work now, we'll pay
you later' tactics.

———————— References ————————

After the interview, should you be the most promising candidate, the employers will check your references. By that time they are almost certain that you are the person for the job and a reference check is the last obstacle on the way to your new position.

Written references

Most people ask for a written reference before they leave the company. Some references are purely stating the period of employment, job title and, sometimes, basic duties. They don't address the candidate's performance, quality of work, personality, strong and weak points or anything similar. That type of reference can serve purely as a documental evidence that you were employed, who your employer was and how long you stayed there. Potential employers are not very interested in that type of reference.

A written reference that provides an employer's view of a former employee's skills, performance and achievements is much more useful to your new (still potential) employer. However, there are some differences. A reference typed on personal stationery gets less credence from employers than on the letter-head of a firm. The employer's view is that in the latter case the opinion is not purely the writer's, but reflects the views of the whole firm. The referee puts his company's credibility behind his opinion.

Some companies have policies that don't allow references to be typed on the company's letter-heads. In that case, you can either ask your former boss to add a remark to a reference, explaining the fact, or you can explain it yourself to prospective employers.

There is only one flaw in the whole business with written references, the flaw that seriously undermines their values: the prospective employers know that every written reference will be a favourable one. I haven't heard of a boss who would write a bad reference and then hand it to the departing employee. The worst that can happen is that your boss may refuse to write you a reference.

Telephone references

Telephone reference checks are regarded by employers as more revealing. When they talk to your former bosses they look for reluctance or hesitancy on the referee's part. It is much more difficult to praise people in person than in written form.

The name of the referee will always be given to a prospective employer by a candidate. By choosing a loyal referee, candidates try to increase their chances of passing the reference checks. But, quite often, employers want to talk to another person who knows the candidate as well, not only to the nominated referee. By using this trick, employers get a 'second opinion', which is usually less favourable, owing to the fact that the second referee wasn't selected by the candidate.

Interviewer's tactics

When your interviewer, or a person who has to check your references, speaks to your former employer, some of the following 'hard' questions will be used (if they do their job properly):

* Would you employ him/her again without hesitation?
* The job we are recruiting for is very challenging. It needs a person with strong _____ skills. Do you really think he/she has what it takes?
* What was the candidate's reason for leaving your company?
* What did the candidate achieve while working for you? Did he/she meet the criteria required for the job?
* What plans did you have for the candidate? Had he/she stayed with your company, would you have promoted him/her or terminated his/her employment?

In a nutshell, the interviewer will tend to probe deep into your relationship with your former employers, to gather as much information as possible on your past performance.

How to get a good reference

Don't burn your bridges. Always part on friendly terms. Write a polite resignation letter and praise your former employer for the encouragement you were given, the opportunities you had and all the nice things they did for you.

When you leave, keep cultivating relationships with your former employers. You will need them to get your next job, and the next one, and the next one . . . If possible, visit them from time to time, displaying interest in them. Send Christmas cards and regularly keep in touch over the phone.

Also, don't rely on just one referee. If he or she leaves the company, the prospective employers will certainly talk to someone else who is still there, and that person may not like you, or know you, or who knows what. Cultivate a 'substitute referee' who can help you with a good reference.

Paperwork

A verbal contract isn't worth the paper it's written on.

Samuel Goldwyn, attributed

Employment contracts

What is a contract of employment? It is an agreement between an employer and an employee that stipulates every part of the employment relationship, either explicitly or implicitly. The strange aspect of the whole situation is that even if you don't sign a piece of paper with a title 'Contract of Employment', a contract nevertheless exists.

That means that an employment contract can be written, oral or implied! This is the beauty of so called 'Common Law'. Whichever way you look at it, beware (*Caveat Emptor*)!

The best strategy is to get a written job offer. Once you accept the offer by signing it, it becomes a valid mutually binding contract of employment. These days, most employers will send you a written job offer by mail. You will be given a few days to think about it, either reject it or sign it and return it to the employer.

Should you wish to add some clauses to an employment offer, ring the employer or go to see them personally to discuss the issue. Once you sign on a dotted line, you have to play by the rules you've agreed upon. Be persistent. Don't believe their usual story, such as 'We would have to retype the letter and wait for the General Manager to return from overseas/Dallas/Zanzibar/hospital to sign it'. If you can negotiate a better deal for yourself, go for it. Not many employers would withdraw a job offer if you make any additional requests. They don't like guerilla fighters, but they respect people who stand up for themselves.

So what should a properly written job offer contain?

- your title and basic job duties;
- your place of work – department, location, branch or alike;
- your working hours;
- your salary, including overtime rates and bonuses or allowances;
- the procedure for payment of salaries or wages;
- the name and title of your immediate superior;
- the day on which employment commences;
- the validity period of the offer (usually seven days);
- the name, address and telephone number of a person who can give you further information and clarify any point or answer any question you may have.

If you have any queries and there is no contact name on the offer, ring the person who interviewed you or the person who signed the offer, and ask for clarification.

Job descriptions

Job descriptions are a typical bureaucratic invention. In a modern working environment where jobs are constantly changing in nature, job descriptions belong in the past.

> *At best, a job description freezes the job as the writer understood it at a particular instant in the past. At worst, they're prepared by personnel people who can't write and don't understand the jobs. Then they are not only expensive to prepare and regularly revise, but they're important morale-sappers.*

> Robert Townsend, *Up The Organisation*

Job descriptions in most cases serve as an additional guarantee to the employers that you will perform any task they ask you to, providing it's listed in the description. So, carefully analyse the document and question the inappropriate tasks, or you may end up punching data into the computer or doing the foreman's job instead of the higher duties for which you believed you were employed.

8

ADITIONAL TACTICS

This chapter is dedicated to people who are in some way disadvantaged in the interviewing process. The reasons for those disadvantages are different, the consequences differ from case to case, too. However, there are many common problems that those job-seekers face.

The most interesting phenomenon among today's disadvantaged groups is the mutual blaming. Natives blame migrants for accepting lower wages and taking 'their' jobs. Migrants complain that employers discriminate against them. Young women blame older, married women for their inability to find jobs, while older women say the employers favour young girls because they do the same jobs for far less money. Victims against victims.

—— For minorities and immigrants ——

Experience is not what happens to you. It is what you do with what happens to you.

Aldous Huxley

The problem

Discrimination of some kind is a part of everyday life for many job hunters. The high unemployment rate for immigrants and minorities is a good indication that old habits and prejudices die hard.

Some recruitment consultants openly and bluntly admit that immigrants, mainly from South-East Asia and India with the same qualifications as their English, Australian or American counterparts do not even have a look-in at the moment. Employers select people with whom they feel they can relate, and in many cases a candidate's résumé is dismissed because of the foreign name on the front page.

Some (or most?) managers do not have the tolerance, patience or broad views that are necessary to deal with employees of different nationalities or backgrounds. Familiarity breeds familiarity. The common excuse for such an attitude is that famous exclaimer that 'local experience is necessary'.

Some lucrative employers realise that most migrants have good skills and a high work ethic, and they abuse that fact. Most migrants are keen to work hard and are committed to their jobs, which leaves them open to exploitation. Due to the lack of knowledge of local conditions and various unwritten rules and employers' tricks and tactics, they are prepared to accept less attractive jobs and lower wages.

Before we take a look at the guerilla tactics that could be used to overcome the problems mentioned above, let's define the criteria that make you a minority. At the first level, two things are obvious: the colour of your skin and your accent. Your background comes next, with details such as your nationality, age, the schools and universities you attended, your family history, etc. These are less important and can be concealed.

Guerilla tactics

So, what could be done about all this? Unfortunately, it's very hard to change people's attitude, so the only possible tactic is 'If you can't beat them, join them'. Sounds like a cliché, but here it is in a nutshell:

- Translate all your documents, diplomas, certificates and references to English and get them verified.
- Put a lot of effort into the preparation of your résumé. If necessary, use outside help (and any help available). Make sure there are no spelling mistakes, no grammatical or syntax errors.
- Improve your English. The better your communication skills, the greater your chances of getting a job.
- If necessary, change your name. It may seem too drastic, but it will at least get you through the first round (when interviewers discard most résumés with foreign names on them) and let you have a fair go. I may be wrong, but I'm convinced that my Serbian name cost me at least a couple of attractive jobs in the past.
- Dress the way local people dress and behave the way they behave. From the moment you apply for the job, try to eliminate old ethnic habits and constraints. Always project sincerity, integrity and a 'globetrotter' image. You have been there and you have done it all. Many people never leave their native country and admire (or at least envy) people who have travelled.
- Study the local job market and the way recruiters and managers think and work, analyse various companies, their attitudes and philosophies. Read self-improvement books, trade magazines and newspaper advertisements and build your database for future job opportunities. Make a folder for each of the big employers. That will help you determine their way of thinking and recruiting.

For women

The problem

> *Whatever women do they must do twice as well as men to be thought half as good. Luckily this is not difficult.*
>
> Charlotte Vitton in M. Rogers, *Contradictory Quotations*

Global society is undergoing a steady demographic change. The biggest change has certainly been in the area of female employment. More and more women are entering the work force or returning to part-time or even full-time employment after the 'domestic' period of starting a family.

Slowly, employers are changing their attitudes and prejudices towards women. Equal Opportunity policies are paving the way towards equality in treatment and pay between men and women. However, women are still not equal with men when it comes to employer's preferences and salary levels. Men are generally paid more than women who perform the same duties.

> *Part of the problem probably lies with women themselves, due to their timidity and lack of energetic approach to job hunting, and later in the work environment.*

A recent study in the USA, which questioned 3347 undergraduates at six of the country's most prestigious universities, found that female students, on average, had lower self-esteem and lower aspirations than their male counterparts.

Re-entering the work force

If you belong to the growing group of women who are returning to part-time or full-time employment after a few years spent at home raising a family, you may find yourself disadvantaged in comparison with your competitors for the same jobs. Although you may not have relevant job experience, think about the skills and experience gained at home, in community service and in various club activities, that can be related to the requirements of the position you are applying for.

The interviewer's fears about women

- They will get married and leave the company; get pregnant and leave; or follow their husbands and leave. In any case, they will leave soon and we'll have to invest time and money again to recruit another person.

- Women are too emotional; they can't control their emotions; they are often depressed and moody; they burst into tears under the slightest pressure or stress.
- They are not able to operate in the man's world, which is ruthless and competitive.
- They cannot fit into male teams. They don't share the same values. They will add an element of sexuality in the team and spoil the male-to-male relationships.
- They don't work as hard as men do, they are not dedicated to their jobs as men are. They view their jobs as places to meet their future husbands.

If you are a woman, you have an additional task in front of you: to convince interviewers that the fears they may have are without foundation, and that you can do your job as well as any man could, if not better.

— For school leavers and graduates —

I have never let my schooling interfere with my education.

Mark Twain

The mistakes graduates make

For those of you who are looking for the first job in 'the real world', there are just a few important points to remember. The fact is that you will never have more control over the hiring process than in the beginning. That means you should not do what most graduates do:

- They send dozens of résumés to every possible employer they can think of and pray for some response. Due to the buyer's market they place themselves at the market's mercy.
- In selecting an employer they go for quick results and forget about long-term interests. They pay too much attention to starting salaries and benefits.

- They don't market and promote themselves properly, so some employers get them very cheap. Under the pretext of gaining experience, they perform work that would cost the employers much more had it been carried out by experienced professionals. Cheap labour? Maybe.

Young people, fresh out of college or university, are the ones with greatest expectations and greatest potential, yet they are the ones that most companies tend to neglect so often. When such smart and ambitious employees (usually thrown into an entry level position and paid less than a cleaner) leave after a year or two for greener pastures, the employers are puzzled. For some strange reason they don't treat their employees as an investment. They don't train them properly or challenge them with projects that are beneficial to both employer and employee.

Some employers realise the pitfalls and expenses involved in losing talented young people and stretch them to their limits. These are the companies you should aim for. To get a job with them, you'll have to do your homework properly.

Guerilla tactics

With recent graduates, most companies look for signs of achievements, not only academic ones, such as scholarships, but also a business approach, self-discipline and election to leadership positions. You have to convince the employers that your academic success is the best indicator of your abilities and the sign of all great things you can do for them.

These are some tips and strategies that every young achiever should consider:

- Select a company before it selects you. Be a chooser, not a beggar. Do your personal balance sheet properly and get to know yourself. Know what you want and devise a plan that will help you get it.
- Never stop learning. Be a student forever. When you finish school or graduate, the real learning process starts. Sounds strange, but it tells you something about the quality of today's education.
- Expect to succeed. Adopt a positive attitude. Despite all doom and gloom, feel confident in yourself, your abilities and the likelihood of

success. Learn as much as possible, as soon as possible. Time is a precious asset, since it's limited. We all have just a certain number of years to live, so don't procrastinate and waste them.

- Take your career in your own hands. Be your own union. Nobody can protect your interests better than you can, yourself. Learn everything about your job as quickly as possible, then about the jobs your colleagues are doing, and about your boss's job, too. Do that, and you will be sitting in his chair sooner than you think.

- Use every opportunity to promote yourself. Be visible and make sure everybody knows when you do a good job. Market yourself aggressively. Attend seminars, conferences, product and trade shows, exhibitions, displays.

- Always keep a hidden ace up your sleeve. A cushion to fall on is a nice thing to have. Keep your options open. Don't overspecialise. Be universal and flexible. Cultivate your business relationships. If you ever lose your job, for any reason, there is a great chance that one of your business contacts may offer you another. Make sure you're ready when the opportunity knocks.

—— For people changing careers ——

Try another profession. Any other.

Head Instructor at *John Murray Anderson Drama School* to
Lucille Ball

The performance of an employee is not a very accurate indicator of how he feels about his job, the company and his achievements. Some people do great jobs in the areas they are not really interested in. Their talent, discipline and hard work lead to good performance, but their real interests are somewhere else.

Most people who have changed their careers admit that there was a cost to achieving that change. Most of them had to face a considerable cut in income, at least initially. Some of them never caught up with their earnings in the old job, but they were much happier for doing things they really liked.

If you think about career turnaround, you really have to analyse yourself thoroughly. You've got to know what your strengths and weaknesses are, and whether they will match the goals you want to achieve. Whatever you do, think twice before you make such an important decision. Keep in mind that grass always *looks* greener on the other side of a fence.

——— For the unemployed ———

Being unemployed becomes reality for more and more people every day. Thousands of jobs are disappearing overnight as companies' fight one of the worst recessions ever. In their battle to become lean and mean, people from various backgrounds, different industries, and with all sorts of qualifications, find themselves on the streets. They are labourers, tradesmen, engineers, managers. Nobody's job is safe, fear and uncertainty become part of our lives.

> *In comparison with people who are employed*
> *and want to change jobs, unemployed job*
> *hunters are definitely disadvantaged, due mostly*
> *to the prevalent employers' misconceptions.*

There is a view among employers that the people who are already employed would perform better in a job and some employment consultants claim that 80 to 90 per cent of the candidates taken by their clients were already in jobs. The fact that someone has been out of work for a long time can cast doubt in the mind of the employer about the overall quality of the applicant.

An additional difficulty that people with higher degrees quite often face is a definite reluctance among employers who are not engaged in research to employ them. They suspect that type of employee will move on as soon as positions that suit their skills better become available. In addition, some managers feel uncomfortable working with people who are more qualified and possibly smarter than themselves. This could simply be called being over-qualified for the job.

Self-esteem

The biggest problem for unemployed job seekers is the constant erosion of their self-esteem. They cannot escape the feeling of inferiority among people with regular employment, even though they may realise that their skills, knowledge and intelligence are far from inferior. The longer they are out of work, the worse it is for their morale. The first step towards consolidation is to boost your morale and self-esteem.

If you are selling yourself to a prospective employer you cannot allow your morale to drop, because there will be many other candidates who have the confidence and self-esteem to be successful. Think positive, think optimism, growth and success.

My advice to unemployed people is very simple:

> *Be a future-orientated person. Don't keep dwelling upon the past. The past won't get you employed.*

Voluntary work

One of the options open to the unemployed is voluntary work. Should you opt for that approach, the first thing you should do is consider a few places where you want to work and offer your services to those employers. If successful, this will enable you to gain new skills and significantly increase your chances of getting a paid job.

In addition, voluntary work will help you build your spirits and maintain a positive mental attitude. It will keep you in contact with the working environment and serve as a credential, highly regarded by prospective employers. In competing with couch potatoes, who have been spending their time at home, watching midday soaps and waiting for employers to call them should the vacancy arise, you will be a clear winner.

If you are good at what you are doing, the whole situation will only be temporary. It is very likely that some sort of remuneration will be offered initially, such as free meals, bus or train fares, etc. As you go along and keep doing a good job for them, your chances of getting a permanent job will multiply. A foot in the door can mean: 'The job is yours!'

For those of you who are unemployed and manage to get a job interview, the important point to remember is to explain your particular case to the interviewer. Don't hide anything or bend the facts. If your job was made redundant and you had to take the company's retrenchment package, that wasn't your fault and should have no impact on your ability to perform in the job for which you are being interviewed.

— For interviewing while employed —

Do what you can, with what you can, where you are.

Theodore Roosevelt, Ex-President of the USA

The reason

So, day by day, your dissatisfaction grows. You are underpaid, or missed a promotion or a pay rise, your boss doesn't respect you, your co-workers are backstabbing you, your job is a bore, you disagree with the company's policies and rules. To cut a long story short: you want to get out.

It makes me very sad to see young, educated, hard-working and ambitious people unemployed or working for peanuts, while other, less educated and less productive people with almost no abilities or skills make a very good living while contributing nothing towards the common good. If you belong to the first group, read the rest of this chapter very carefully.

Guerilla tactics for underpaid professionals

If you have invested large amounts of time and money to get a diploma or a degree and to advance to the professional level, you should be ferociously determined to get your investment back and with interest. From the employers and clients, of course.

Lawyers and doctors have been practising this for years. Other professionals, such as engineers, architects or scientists, have even more rights to do so, yet, they are marginalised and sadly neglected. This is my advice to these job hunters:

- There is no union that protects your interests, therefore, the onus is on you to protect what you have and acquire what you want. The end usually justifies the means.
- Practise professional courtesy. Make life easier for other members of your profession and for yourself. Never criticise or badmouth your colleagues. By helping make your profession recognised and appreciated you strengthen your own position tremendously.
- Project a busy and professional attitude. Let people (and employers) realise that your time is valuable and that your expectations are high. Be a no-nonsense person. Don't let them fool you and take you for granted.
- Learn not only about your job, but as much as possible about other people's jobs. That will give you an edge in dealings with them, broaden your horizons and prepare you for the top jobs.
- Be visible and market yourself. If your boss doesn't recognise your talents, be sure that his competitors will. If your boss is your obstacle to moving up, change your boss. Don't waste time.
- Whatever you do, believe in yourself. Remember the famous words: 'Day by day in every way I'm getting better and better' (Emile Coue, the author of *Self-mastery Through Autosuggestion*). The power of autosuggestion is enormous. Think positive, think big.
- Plan to win. The one element that stands out most clearly among high achievers is their strong belief in their success. They plan to win! From now on, I'm sure, you'll plan to win, too.

*If your boss doesn't recognise your talents, be
sure that his competitors will.*

Time constraints

Time is the biggest problem for the job seekers who are still employed. It
isn't easy to enquire about jobs and attend interviews while working from
8 to 5. But, there are some ways to overcome this obstacle. First of all,
use your weekends for writing job applications, doing your research on
employers and mastering your interviewing skills. Use your lunch hours
for enquiries and other telephone contacts with employers.

If you have an appointment for an interview in the same town, take a day
off, if you can, preferably paid. If this is not possible, arrange an interview
for late afternoon, or Saturday morning. Most managers and recruiters
work long hours and Saturdays, and will accommodate their plans to meet
a promising candidate. If the position you are interested in is a good
distance away, take two or more days off. Use your annual leave. Specify
the simple reason: Personal business.

Using your sick leave is another option. Most companies have a policy
that for up to two days of sickness no medical certificate is necessary. Be
careful when using sickness as excuse, for there is always a chance that
someone you know may see you looking smart and business-like while
you were supposed to be lying ill in bed.

Feeling guilty

Some of you may feel guilty when looking for a job while still employed. I
always felt the same. Then I realised that many other people were doing
the same, even my boss and his manager. It is common practice in
Western society. Employers have the right to terminate your employment at any time, if they can justify their decision. That justification could
be poor performance (sacking) or redundancy (retrenchment).

They can prepare for that situation by training your replacement and by
transferring some or all of your duties to your colleagues. You, an
employee, have similar rights in protecting yourself from losing your job

and in advancing your career. You also have the right to quit at any time and to prepare for the act of quitting through applying for other jobs and through interviewing with other employers.

Keeping your mouth shut

There is one golden rule to be remembered no matter what you do or what your job hunting strategies are: never tell anybody that you are looking for a job. The only exceptions are the people who can help you in the process. Most people cannot keep a secret, and the last thing you want is for your employer to find out that you are looking for a better job. So, don't trust anyone.

Never apply for a position if the advertisement gives only a post office box number. It could be a bogus advertisement and your application may end up in the wrong hands or your name may appear on all mail order lists imaginable. Some less-reputable mail order companies do that. So do employers, in order to 'probe' the market.

Employment agencies

Even employment agencies should not be trusted. There is a great chance that your résumé will finish on your employer's desk, through who knows what channels. Employment consultants are more loyal to employers, because it's the employers who pay their commission. Candidates are a commodity, nothing more and nothing less.

In some cases, the existence of employment agencies can be justified. They bring employers and job hunters together. Most of the time, however, employers use personnel consultants to do their job for them, because they either have no time or expertise to select people or because they think that 'professional' head-hunters would do a better job than they would. I consider that a big mistake. It not only costs them money, but they rely on others to select the right person for the job.

Alternative: write to potential employers directly. Do your own marketing. You'll create a much better impression if you directly approach the company you are interested in, for you display initiative and resilience.

Skip the middle men. Employers pay them to find the candidates, so, naturally, they must get that money back from somebody. That somebody is you.

Don't quit until you've got that other job. Personnel departments, like banks, deal only with people who don't need them.

Robert Townsend, *Up The Organization*

9
—— FINAL ADVICE ——

Job hunting is a game. Sometimes you win, sometimes you lose. It is a different game than, say, the Olympic Games, where the motto is to participate. In job hunting, you should play to win. Winning is the most important thing in life and nothing else can be compared with that feeling.

On the other hand, losing is not necessarily bad, either. It should teach you how to improve your performance and win more often. Smart people learn from their mistakes, analyse them and never repeat the same mistake twice. Top performers learn from other people's mistakes. That should be your goal, too.

Don't despair if your first interviews turn out to be failures. Keep trying.

People say: 'Practice makes perfect'. I would add to that: 'Perfect practice makes perfect'. The best way to practise is to apply for some jobs you don't really want or need, just to get as much experience in interviewing as possible. When the big opportunity comes up you'll be ready to use that experience. That will give you a big advantage over your competitors. They will lack practice and knowledge of the interviewing process. They will be uneasy, nervous and will sell their abilities short.

You, on the other hand, will be 'battle-hardened'. You will recognise questions, fears, tricks and traps and use advanced tactics, proven in your previous interviews.

To get the job you want and to steer your career in the right direction, you must take one step at a time, but each step should lead you to your final goal: success. Success is a relative word, the meaning of it varies from person to person. But, to me, there is only one definition of real success: to be able to spend your life the way **you** want!

There are two possible paths for career advancement. In the first, you jump around from company to company. If you learn quickly, know how to make new friends, handle people and lever your skills and knowledge into better positions, this path is for you. You have to keep your eyes and ears open, keep in touch with people, regularly refresh your knowledge, upgrade your existing skills and acquire new ones.

The alternative approach is to grow within one company. Big players are particularly suitable for this method. In some cases just by staying with the employer long enough you can get to the top. Something like the army logic. This takes patience and persistence. You have to master the corporate games and office politics. This is probably the more difficult path, especially in today's business climate.

I consider career leapfrogging the quickest way to get to the top. Days of loyalty to one employer, one idea or one product are gone and forgotten. Your employer is not loyal to you: you are on a few weeks' notice. That's his loyalty. So why should you be loyal to your employer?

This is all that the job interview is: a sales presentation. It is the only sales presentation where the product sells itself. That product is you.

——— At the end ———

Advice is judged by results, not by intentions.

CICERO, *Ad Atticum IX*

The interviewing tactics you've learned in this book should prove useful in your current and future job-hunting endeavours. However, the final results will depend not only on your skills, but also on the skills of the people interviewing you. Some amateurish interviewers will be steam-rolled by the use of your advanced strategies. Some experienced professionals, on the other hand, will be able to recognise you as a 'professional interviewee' and will put more effort in evaluating you.

Some of them will read this book, I guess, and come up with counter-measures for neutralising your efforts. But, don't despair. Not all of them are so professional and astute to figure you out.

Looking for a job and employment interviewing is one of the loneliest, most difficult and most frustrating businesses in the world. Many times you'll feel down and out, you'll question your abilities, lose your self-confidence, feel discouraged and disillusioned. To achieve your goal you'll have to fight all those negative thoughts and feelings. I cannot stress enough how important it is to maintain a positive attitude. If you don't believe in yourself, nobody will. Apart from believing in your own abilities, you'll need stamina, perseverance and hard work. And a bit of luck, of course.

> *I'm a great believer in luck, and the harder I work, the*
> *luckier I get.*
>
> Stephen Leacock, Canadian Humorist

So, at the end of our job-hunting and interviewing journey, I hope I have given you a better idea of how recruiters think and what they want to hear at a job interview. The last thing I can do for you is wish you all the best in your current and future efforts in finding the 'top job' you deserve. Thank you for reading this book.